HAWKS
of the
HADHRAMAUT

By the same author

Warlords of Oman

HAWKS
of the
HADHRAMAUT

P. S. ALLFREE

ROBERT HALE · LONDON

© P.S. Allfree 1967
First published in Great Britain 1967
Paperback edition 2013

ISBN 978-0-7198-0738-1

Robert Hale Limited
Clerkenwell House
Clerkenwell Green
London EC1R 0HT

www.halebooks.com

The right of P.S. Allfree to be identified as author of this
work has been asserted by him in accordance
with the Copyright, Designs and Patents Act 1988

A catalogue record for this book is available from the British Library

2   4   6   8   10   9   7   5   3   1

Printed and bound by MPG Books Group, Bodmin and King's Lynn

Contents

To my wife

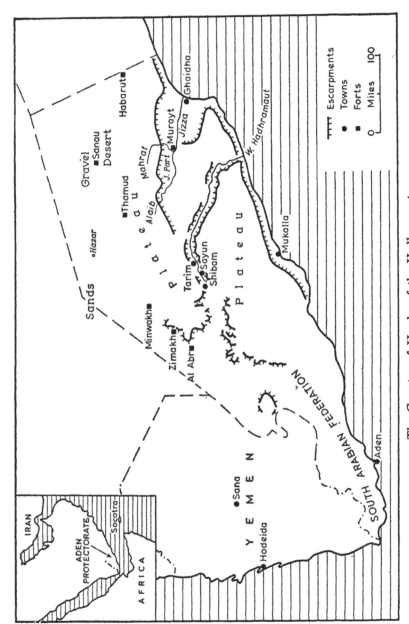

The Country of Hawks of the Hadhramaut

ONE

Land of Prophets

RED, white and blue billowed splendid against a sunlit sky. All in a blinding shimmer beneath this banner of Britannic might stood a tall white façade, garnished with black woodwork round windows, doors, and balconies, emblazoned with the royal arms, and crowned with three dazzling square white turrets. Behind it rose a stark dun crag holding up a crumbling rock-built watch-tower. Around it clustered peeling office buildings of brown stone, vibrant with heat. Beside the grand and pillared entrance paced a brown soldier, swishing in a calf-length robe of crisp snow-white. He wore a long red head-dress dangling down his back, a broad red cummerbund, a short black beard.

He halted as we drew up, stamped silently with soft brown soles, presented arms. From somewhere behind a wood-framed balcony came gliding the medieval strains of Vivaldi: or it might have been Corelli.

Our Land-Rover stopped and out of a side door in the porch popped a pale man, with a long Oxford face and sleek hair. He smiled a pallid welcome and his long Oxford voice formulated a greeting.

" So pleased to see you. Had a good trip down?"

I had arrived.

This was Mukalla: seat of His Highness the Sultan of the Qaiti State; more precisely, the crystalline mansion with the flag on top was the Residency, wherein resided a gentleman called the Resident Adviser and British Agent—known, for reasons of economy, as the R.A. The wan Oxford face belonged to an Assistant Adviser. The flap-footed sentry was an Arab soldier of the Hadhramaut Bedouin Legion. In a nutshell, I was in the East Aden Protectorate.

As I had arrived at lunch-time my new friend led me up some clattering wooden stairs to an anteroom on the first floor, where he told me, " the Ah Ray will see you soon." The walls were heavy with pompous portraits. Wisps of Venetian melody floated daintily from a private chamber. Somebody was playing the violin, treating himself and anybody else who might be around to a consummate rendering of some intricate classical air. I remembered some things I had heard about Arthur Watts, the reigning R.A.: that he had come to Aden early in the war as a humble Artillery sergeant, and was now judged one of the foremost practical Arabic scholars outside the Arab race; that he was one of the wiliest politicians and diplomats since Talleyrand and Metternich, and had been reckoned a musician of potential maestro calibre; and that he abhorred military men. I was thankful that I had shed the trappings of the profession I had been practising until the very day before, though a certain martial tang still clung to my person like the smell of tar to a sailor—I winced whenever my companion addressed me as " major ", a hangover from his previous official correspondence with me.

For the last four and a half years I had been a mercenary in the service of the Sultan of Muscat and Oman, who was endeavouring to discipline a rebellious subject-prince with the assistance of a small band of British free-lances. Life with the Sultan was outlandish enough, and at times dangerous enough, to slake most of the lust for the exotic that had originally lured me to Oman; but while there I had heard tales, and seen pictures, of what seemed an even more extravagant romantic land, where there was not just one Sultan but three. There, I learnt, where the great gorge of the Hadhramaut gnawed its way between thousand-foot rose-red cliffs, slumbered an antique civilisation stretching back to the days of Noah, fantastic with towering cities and splendid palaces and formidable bearded men. And on the fringes of this golden country lay the Great Desert of Arabia, the Empty Quarter, where the real Arabs roamed—the tribes of Rashid and Amer, the dwellers in tents, the Bedouin.

It was, of course, a dream: but with my appetite for Arabia ungorged, and my mouth watering for these new wonders, I resigned from the Sultan's army and applied to the Aden Government for a post.

For south and west of Muscat a huge wedge of Arabia was tinted pink on our maps. Inside this enclave the Sultans and Sheikhs held court but the Colonial Office held sway. To reach my goal I must join the Colonial Service. This I did. I received a letter, embossed with the royal arms, inviting me to assume the duties and title of Assistant Adviser to the Resident Adviser and British Agent. I said good-bye to my old friends who soldiered on in Muscat, hitched a lift on an Aden-bound R.A.F. transport, and here I was, awaiting my introduction to Arthur Watts while Vivaldi fiddled to his contrapuntal close.

The Aden Protectorate's ruddy complexion was more a geographer's simplification of Imperial politics than a true reflection of the territory's status. It was in no sense a colony, as Aden Town was; nor, while dubbed a protectorate, was it controlled by Britain to anything like the degree of other protectorates like the old Uganda or Nyasaland. The title of the chief British official in Mukalla represented the intention, if not the final evolution, of British policy there: the handful of pale-faced civil servants played an advisory, not an executive rôle. The sceptres of the several States—in theory, sovereign and free—were brandished firmly, if sometimes erratically, in the hands of the hereditary Sultans.

But these gentry were endowed with British advice, a bounty made available to them generously: indeed, so zealous was Whitehall in the dissemination of its counsel, that there was a clause in each Sultan's treaty with Her Majesty which compelled him to accept that advice. So, throughout the years, Sultans have been advised to establish schools, to refrain from war, to issue stamps; and, when refractory, Sultans had been known to receive advice to abdicate.

The fountain-head of this ineluctable tutelage, for the Eastern Protectorate, lay in the Residency at Mukalla.

The position of this " advice ", and of the still modest but ominously burgeoning advisory staff, was by the time I arrived to join in the game becoming distinctly uncomfortable; because the pretence that compulsory advice is less authoritarian than mandatory rule was increasingly difficult to maintain against a clamorous crescendo of nationalism. In vain did the adviser shrug his shoulders and say, " I am only here to advise "—all the shortcomings of the land and its Government were inevitably laid firmly at the adviser's door; and, being only a counsellor, he could earn little credit for all the genuine progress which he urged. If he advised too hard, or particularly if he put on his full-dress uniform to enounce " official " —i.e. compulsory—advice to a Sultan, he was behaving like a Victorian pro-consul. If he refrained from exerting his legitimate powers on some minor matter of popular concern, he was guilty of perfidious laxity. It was an unenviable position. Even the most virulent Cairo-schooled radicals had been heard to say that they would prefer direct imperial rule to this halfhearted compromise between feudal sovereignty and colonial subjection. But the origins of this unhappy hybrid lie deep in the sardonic bosom of the muse of History.

The distinguishing feature of the Protectorate is a desolate windswept tableland of bare brown stone, three or four hundred miles across, five or six thousand feet high, flanking the coast east of Aden and dipping drearily into the red-grey desert of the Empty Quarter. Level and drab as a mud-flat, with here and there a solitary mesa lifting from the wilderness, this dead upland stretches blankly to the horizon, like the very roof of the world. Ages of erosion have etched deep into the petrified waste, grinding out a complex of dry water-courses, relics of the days of the European Ice Age when Arabia was deluged by centuries of tropical rain. These ravines gouge their way deeper and deeper through the layers of stone, from the north and from the south, to join—like ribs to a spine—the colossal trunk-gorge which slices through the plateau some thousand feet below its surface. Here, sheltered in the depths of a howling desert, lies the great valley of the Hadhramaut, leading from the green and misty hills of the Yemen to the shores of the Gulf of Aden.

One hundred naked miles from the sea, and with nothing beyond but a continent of dead rock and range upon parallel range of towering sand-dunes, the valley has spawned a civilisation of its own, as isolated from the rest of mankind as an island in mid-ocean. The canyon is fertile: water underlies the deep silt floor.

The earliest visitors, according to legend, were giants from the days of Noah. According to archaeology, its first human inhabitants were men of the Stone Age, who fashioned tools and weapons from the flints in the rock and left their indestructible litter as tokens of their passing. The first historical people to plant their footprints here were the Himyarites: a race of Semitic stock, related to the subjects of Balkis Queen of Sheba who reigned in nearby Yemen.

Tradition puts the Koranic prophets Saleh and Hud in the Hadhramaut and its embracing sands. The name " Hadhramaut "—echoing two Arabic words for " presence " and " death "—suggests the Valley of the Shadow of Death. Bible, Koran, history and legend, blend mistily in the past of this strange country.

The people to whom the prophet Saleh, grandson of Noah, brought the message of the One God, and who rejected him, were destroyed—says the Koran—by a tidal wave of sand, and submerged beneath the great hills. There are stories still told of buried cities smothered beneath five hundred feet of desert dunes, and there are ancient paths and tracks in the wilderness which have no purpose or meaning unless they lead to some long-obliterated market place. Hud, the patron saint of the Hadhramaut, was Saleh's son, called Eber in our Bible. His grave is tucked into a ledge half-way up the cliff, tenderly tended and sparkling with whitewash. Inside is Hud's sarcophagus. It is about thirty feet long. Saleh's tomb lies in a deep tributary of the Hadhramaut, and is still—as it has been for a hundred generations—an object of pilgrimage. It is over twenty feet long . . . "there were giants in the earth in those days " . . . nobody knows what is really preserved in these gigantic sepulchres.

The history of the coming of the Arabs is obscure. Virile nomads, what they found—of architecture, of sculpture, of civilisation—they destroyed, like the Huns in Europe. The Hadhramaut is rich in antique ruins. There are remnants of fine masonry, pagan images, inscriptions in the angular Himyaritic script; there are collapsed fortresses, of a structural excellence that the Arabs since have never even tried to emulate. The relics of Himyar stand in the Hadhramaut as the ruins of ancient Greece and Rome stand today in Europe —mute cenotaphs of a culture, magnificent but effete, sacrificed to a more muscular barbarity.

The nineteen or twenty centuries following the collapse of the old civilisation display a shifting pattern of tribal warfare, of Sultanates blossoming, blooming, decaying; of tribes flourishing, dominating, all-powerful, then bowing before another. The victorious peoples settled fatly in the valley, the vanquished fled to the desert for refuge and became wanderers —the Bedouin. There were many changes of fortune.

In the Middle Ages came the greatest conqueror of all: Badr bu Tuwairiq led his tribe of Kathir bursting in from the far north-east and overran almost the whole of south Arabia. When this deluge of conquest had flooded the Hadhramaut, it settled, stagnated, finally dissipated, leaving here and there the scattered communities of Kathir which still exist today like rock pools at low tide. The Kathiri Sultan, who rules a large part of the central Hadhramaut gorge, is the living monument of this once great empire.

Slowly the cauldron of anarchy congealed. The remains of the aborigines, penned in their inaccessible refuge between cliff and sea, have maintained their antique language and their contempt for the Arabs whom they look down on to this day as savage interlopers. They are known as the Mahra, a name

related to an old Arabic word for " clever " or " skilful "—
perhaps a pathetic memento of the ancient days when their
civilised ancestors must indeed have seemed " clever " to the
Arab barbarians.

The Mahra now are the most degenerate and primitive of all
the inhabitants of Hadhramaut, but they preserve in their
legends the great era when the whole land was theirs. The
Mahra displaced the Portuguese on Socotra Island. They established there a Sultanate. Gradually the mainland men, wild
as mountain lions, shrugged off the authority of their sea-girt
Sultan and slipped gratefully back into a state of virgin
anarchy. The Sultan of Socotra is the second of the strange trio
of monarchs in the Protectorate, a sovereign whose claim to his
mainland territory—contested with vigour by the Mahra who
live there—was staunchly upheld by the Protecting Power.

The third, and the most powerful, Sultan is the descendant
of a captain of South Arabian mercenaries employed by one
of the parties in a Hadhramaut civil war of the eighteenth
century. The captain remained after winning the war and
established himself as a baron; his successors throve, and
eventually became hereditary rulers of Mukalla and its depen-
dencies. The Qaiti Sultan is the latest scion of this ambitious
military clan. His palace squats like a grossly over-blown sea-
side pier-head opposite the Residency.

During the last century British commercial and maritime
enterprise was changing the face of the world. Aden and its
environs was merely one of a great number of outlandish
places which saw the Union Jack run up, heard the various
and uncouth accents of the English language, and felt in time
the calm of the Pax Britannica. To create an atmosphere of
tranquillity in which to pursue their mercantile interests, the
British entered into a series of peace treaties with the tribes
surrounding the rock of Aden. As year followed year, this inoffensive influence spread in ever-widening concentric circles
up into the savage hinterland. The frontiers of feud and
anarchy were pushed further and further back from the coal-
ing stations, the wharfs, banks and business houses of burgeoning Aden. In due course the spreading ripples lapped as far as

the Hadhramaut, and even Socotra. In the latter half of the nineteenth-century treaties of friendship were signed with the three eastern Sultans. These pacts were later enlarged to include provisions for advice (which, as we have seen, the Sultans were bound to accept), and for protection against the rapacity of their neighbours: which meant in effect that Britain was undertaking, *ipso facto*, the maintenance of peace in the whole wild land.

Nothing else, however, was attempted by the increasingly harassed British pro-consuls to interfere in these remote and inhospitable provinces, until the 1930s. Then the Sultans of Qaiti and Kathir, distressed by the chaotic conditions of their own domains and impressed by the increasing welfare of the protected emirates nearer to Aden colony, petitioned the Governor of Aden to send them an emissary to advise them on putting their houses in order.

The Hadhramaut Sultanates thirty years ago were one huge gangrenous sore: a seething culture of murderous strife, unchecked banditry and mad marauding tribes. Merchants travelled from town to town with privately-enlisted armed guards; the officials of the Sultans dared not set foot outside their capitals without a strong escort of soldiers; whole cities changed hands from Sultan to Sultan and back again. The women of different cities, even now, wear clothes of distinctive hues, blue, red, or saffron, a reminder of those ferocious days when it was a convenience to know which women one could with impunity rape. The tribes were gripped by such a virulent plague of blood-feud that no man knew who was not his mortal enemy.

The Governor agreed to the Sultans' request, and despatched a man called Harold Ingrams who, alone but for his wife and a saintly sage of the Hadhramaut named Abubaker—later knighted by the King-Emperor—undertook the Promethean task of bringing peace to the Protectorate. This, incredibly, he did: virtually single-handed; the Peace of Ingrams is the greatest event in the history of the Hadhramaut, and one of the most extraordinary achievements in the annals of imperialism. The only parts he was unable to settle were the desert, where the Bedouin apparently existed for the sole purpose of killing each other and stealing one another's camels, and the Mahra —whose introspective savagery and inborn hatred of everybody including themselves rendered their country practically impenetrable, let alone pacifiable.

Under this Peace the States of Qaiti and Kathir began to develop. The people, after two thousand years of anarchy and chaos, were able to look about and see what could be done with their fertile but strife-ravaged homeland.

The British Government however did little more to help them until the end of the Second World War, when a number of economic forces had combined to reduce the territory to famine. Aden sent up a strong contingent of officials, with shiploads, plane-loads and lorry-loads of grain, to feed the starving Arabs.

One of the men despatched on this errand was a Sergeant Watts, of the Royal Artillery, who had spent his idle hours in Aden gossiping with waterfront labourers and had perfected his command of the Arabic tongue. He so impressed his superiors that on his demobilisation they invited him to join the Colonial Service and stay in the Hadhramaut. He agreed; and he flourished.

In the years following the War the colonial Government began to take itself more seriously than in the old days, when a Treaty of Protection was enough to add several hundred thousand square miles to the Empire. In Ingrams's day the Adviser had been on his own, dispensing his advice single-handed. Now that official began to sprout: he thrust forth shoots like a blackberry, Assistant Advisers taking root throughout the country, themselves proliferating here and there with Junior Assistant Advisers. Sergeant Watts worked his way brilliantly and musically up the scale until by the time I first made his acquaintance he was Resident Adviser and British Agent in Mukalla: R.A. for short.

The elegant tweedle-deeing soothed itself to a close and the master-fiddler himself came in. I remembered something I had been told by a malicious wag from Mukalla: that every-

B

body there was looking forward to the day when student riots set the town on fire. Then, he said, Arthur Watts could achieve his fulfilment. He could take up his violin and fiddle while Mukalla burnt. But the jest was unjust.

Watts was a curry-coloured man of pneumatic appearance and no pomposity. He was large in all directions and so utterly unassuming that it was only when you heard him discourse on Arabian politics, or discuss some delicate diplomacy in Arabic with a local Richelieu, that you realised in whose presence you were. And then he was impressive.

Within a short time he had also impressed me with my assignment. I had been warned of my job in advance, but in terms so weighed down with officialese that they were flattened. I was to be Assistant Adviser, Northern Deserts, with responsibility for that part of the Protectorate which was not inhabited by a settled population, and for a frontier with Saudi Arabia from the Yemen on the left to Oman on the right. On the official notepaper with the royal arms on top and some secretary's signature on the bottom this intelligence passed unnoticed overhead, eliciting no more than a nod as I read it. But now Watts handed me a map. There was the Protectorate, there was Mukalla on the coast. Winding diagonally and complicatedly across the middle was the Hadhramaut Valley. And the rest, he told me, was mine.

The map was a small one, and the area seemed modest. Then I looked at the scale. One inch on that map represented fifty miles. I calculated. The piece of land where I would work, alone—"your duties," another Assistant Adviser summed them up for me later, "are to make sure that the Northern Deserts do not bother the R.A."—was the size of England, give or take a few thousand square miles.

But what was I to do there?

"Keep the place quiet," said Arthur Watts. "Keep the Bedouin from cutting each other's throats. Stop them waging war with the Yemen and Saudi Arabia. Make sure they have enough water. Settle their quarrels. Keep the trivia of the desert out of my In tray. Oh yes "—he might even have winked —" and don't get on the wrong side of Pat Gray."

TWO

Bedouin Greetings

" BULLETS," they said.

They perched on one foot with their spare legs tucked up and their arms around each other's necks, like a pair of brotherly storks. One had a broad cheese-shaped face, cheerfully wicked eyes and drooping strings of moustaches like a youthful Genghis Khan. The older man had a cluster of whiskers about his mouth, and the eyes of a lizard.

" Shooting," they said in unison.

They wore long shapeless nightshirts of coarse cotton sacking with the merchants' mark still visible through the dirt, and rags of rough wool, like pieces torn from an old rug, wrapped around their heads. Their hands gripped rifles sewn up in fringed leather Davy Crocket cases. From their belts, which were studded with blackened brass cartridge cases and a few live rounds, poked well-honed kitchen knives. Their feet were gnarled roots.

" Murder "—with increasing agitation, but unwavering courtesy.

Jim Ellis knew what they were talking about. I didn't.

Jim Ellis had driven me up to what was to be my home for the next nine or ten months: Al Abr, a little fort stuck comically on top of a rock overlooking a cluster of wells on the edge of the desert. The moment we stopped—before we had time to climb out of the Land-Rover—these two Bedouin came sprinting wildly up to us, arms and feathery rifle-cases waving in the air, shouting unintelligible slogans at the top of their voices.

But Jim just stood there like a cliff and began to shout steadily back at them. Jim Ellis, enormous of bulk and monumentally stable, was more of a mountain than a mere man. He had spent so many years in this desert, among these Arabs, that they looked upon him as something peculiarly their own. He was no mere Political Officer—a creature for which they had small regard, and a thing which, I could see, these two storks had already marked me down to be.

Jim Ellis, with his elephantine carcase, his inexhaustible good nature, his common sense—a match for the wiliest nomad—and his small moustache like a couple of feathers sticking out of a great crimson pillow, was one of the tiny handful of outsiders—Arab or British—whom the Bedouin held in real respect. To be brought to the desert and introduced to the Bedouin by Ellis was like being taken into Sherwood Forest by Little John.

Ellis spoke chattily to our reception committee of two, in a language which might have been Eskimo. I had already spent some eight years on and off in Arabia in charge of Arab soldiers, even doing intelligence work; but this Bedouin *patois* was gibberish to me—rendered no more lucid by Jim's braw Scots voice. Even the names were not what I had been used to: here were no Alis, no Abdullahs, no Mohammeds. The budding Genghis Khan was called Bin Huweil and the black-whiskered lizard was Sarur.

From what little I could glean from the jabbering trio it seemed that Sarur and Bin Huweil had heard shots while peaceably grazing their goats a day's camel-ride away. Such alarming sounds, so near the frontier where prowled their traditional foes, could mean but one thing—a raid. So the urgent pair had galloped post-haste to Al Abr fort to request —no, to demand—the protection of Her Majesty's Government.

" War," they explained.

Within seconds the fort was a bustling beehive as Ellis ordered out a patrol of troops. These were the Hadhramaut Bedouin Legion; the same corps of disciplined wild-cats who, when relieved from the desert, guarded the Mukalla Residency with placid white-gowned ceremony. Out of the little tower they tumbled, a khaki avalanche, clutching rifles and piling helter-skelter into a couple of Land-Rovers, red head-cloths streaming as they scampered past; in a shower of gravelly dust the patrol shot madly bucketing away to the Empty Quarter, to vanish in the hazy north. It all took about four minutes.

"Praise be to God," smiled Sarur and Bin Huweil, still propping themselves up against each other on one leg. They had stood immobile throughout.

"Noo let's goo inside and have a drink," said Jim to me.

"In the first place," Jim was telling me later, "these fellows—the Saar, they call themselves—are about the most rapacious and belligerent of all your future boy-friends." He sipped from a tumbler of whisky held like a thimble between a huge finger and thumb. "And this section of them, led by Sarur, Bin Huweil, and a few others ye'll meet, are the worst of the lot."

We were sitting on hard wooden folding chairs in one of the three tiny cells which added up to my new home—the Rest House, so-called, snuggling under Al Abr fort. Three little closets of dirty white washed stone faced out, through fly-net doors and too few windows, on to a sloping miniature court-yard paved with razor-sharp chunks of ballast. At the bottom right-hand corner sat a square construction which might have been a stove or an incinerator. In fact it contained a hole in the floor and a roll of toilet paper. On the threshold of the courtyard sat a sentry, idly flapping his hand at a crowd of cawing Arabs as though scaring crows.

"Given half a chance," Jim's juggernaut voice rolled on, "these Saar of yours would spend their time raiding across the border among the Saudi tribes; then whenever the Saudis start to get irritated they'd come yammering on your door here asking for the protection of the Brritish!"

I heard wildly revving engines, shouts, scuffling sounds. The patrol had returned. An Arab lieutenant stepped in, white with dust, saluted and reported. The gunmen had been other Saar, ineffectively hunting gazelle. Jim Ellis nodded sagely. " Just keeping us on our toes," he sighed. " One up to Sarur."

Already, though it was only mid-morning in early March the desert heat was prickling my sweat glands and turning my tongue to blotting paper. But Jim's voice was steady as an ocean swell. My hardest but most recurrent task, he said, would be not (as I had imagined) to protect peace-loving shepherds from human wolves, but to prevent my own wolves from ravaging comparatively well-behaved neighbours and then running for the guns of the Legion when they felt blasts of wrath from over the border. This border, to enhance my problem, was merely a straight line on a map, and paid no respect at all to the cherished grazing grounds of the tribes on either side: it sliced across the homelands of Saar, of Saudis, and of Yemenis. . . .

" And there's another headache for ye." Jim tipped the last of his whisky down his throat. " The favourite enemies of your Saar are the Dahm from the Yemen; if anything, more incorrigible raiders than these. We've been trying for years— our people here, and the Yemen Government on their part— to get the two sides to make peace. But there's always one fellow who won't have it. He says he's owed a camel or a blood-debt and he won't accept the truce. The current menace here is Bin Huweil. He's a one-man *casus belli*."

I was regarding with dread the moment when this massive and reassuring tutor would have to depart for his own parish, in the Hadhramaut valley a hundred and fifty miles away. Al Abr itself was clearly no tea-party; but Al Abr was only one tiny nook of the Northern Deserts. There were six such forts, spaced along the frontier on strategic wells, separated by an average of a hundred miles apiece; and every station boasted its own peculiar problems, its special menace, its local *casus belli*. Furthermore Al Abr was the quietest post, the most civilised, for its fort had been established the longest. It dated from 1939. The latest, Habarut in the far north-east, six hundred miles or so away, had only been planted six years ago, in 1956, and was still eyed as an outrageous intrusion by the inhabitants of the area.

Here at Al Abr, at least nobody complained about the fort. The Arabs tended, rather, to abuse the protection it provided, each faction demanding its support for their own cause in every mad dispute.

I was beginning, too, to learn the reason behind the warning Arthur Watts had slipped me, back in Mukalla. " Keep on the right side of Pat Gray," he had said.

Ellis explained that while Arthur Watts, the political supremo, looked to me as his personal representative, in complete charge of all Government resources in the desert, these forces themselves had a different view. The Hadhramaut Bedouin Legion found the garrisons of the six forts, and these two hundred men were the only effective power at my elbow. But their manager was not me. Not at all. I was merely a civilian. Their chief was the Commandant in H.Q. at Mukalla: Pat Gray. To add savour to the dish, Pat Gray was reputed to abominate Political Officers as much as Arthur Watts loathed soldiers.

It would have been quite in order for the fort commander at Al Abr to refuse to send out that patrol at Jim Ellis's behest (and, as it happened, he would have been quite right); he might have referred the requisition by radio to Mukalla. It would have been entirely legitimate if Pat Gray refused, for some perfectly genuine military consideration, and in this case he would have been quite right too. But what was a poor bewildered Political Officer to do?

All I could do, Jim Ellis advised, was just what Arthur Watts had meant—cultivate and maintain close and cordial relations with the soldiers, so that we worked as a team in the desert with no clash of authority or personal animus. Otherwise, he told me, I would have one more enemy to fight during my tour of duty: the Hadhramaut Bedouin Legion.

A beam of hope glimmered through the murk. For one thing, although I was now a civilian on Watts's staff, I had (unlike some of my less happy predecessors) been a soldier hitherto. I could thus expect that Pat Gray would accept me as a fellow human being. Also I could talk to the legionaries in their own barrack-room language, for I was used to Arab troops. Moreover—I congratulated my guardian angel—I knew Pat Gray.

Pat Gray was a large bluff Falstaff with moustaches like mutton chops and an alarmingly brusque manner. He had a disconcerting habit of sweeping an arm out and around in a sudden expansive gesture, which it was wise to duck. He was soldiering in Muscat when I joined the Sultan's army; we had campaigned together against the rebel Imam and became as good friends as a captain and a colonel can be. With Pat Gray behind me I had high hopes of developing a working *entente* with his competent but arrogant Arab officers.

Pat Gray's legionaries were not quite my sole support. At my exclusive disposal stood a devoted band of rascals known as Desert Guards. These were some twenty or thirty stalwarts enrolled from the tribes who habitually water at Al Abr, whose only regular duty was to turn up once a quarter for their pay. They were called out for occasional chores in between pay-days: guiding vehicles through the desert; taking messages to remote chiefs; pursuing malefactors. The leader of this happy band was a humourist called Bin Zaid. He kept chickens. I never knew why, because in his book their flesh was unclean and their eggs were poisonous—and my observations of the diet of these fowl led me to sympathise. But I often heard Bin Zaid clucking and cackling around the fort, gathering in his feathery flock. Once he scared the wits out of me by bursting in on my breakfast, crowing like a raucous cockerel, and waggling the fingers of his right hand over the top of his head in imitation of a cockscomb. . . .

Next day the fatal moment came. Jim Ellis squeezed himself into his Land-Rover and took off for the Hadhramaut. I felt I was dropping the pilot, at the start of a long voyage, with inadequate charts and no crew.

On the first evening after his departure I walked solitarily up the little courtyard from a nose-wrinkling inspection of the wells and opened the door of my day-cell. And there squatting cosily on the floor was a delegation of Saar. All wore the same shaggy sack-cloth and variously-coloured woollen head-rags; each sat in a kind of Buddha pose with the right foot resting over the left thigh. They rose sedately as I blinked into the room. They answered my prim townsman's salutation with carefully imitated primness. I sat down in front of them, cross-legged on the floor, and did my best not to look apprehensive.

I recognised Sarur, reptilian eyes a-twinkle with something I could not interpret. Bin Huweil's moon-shaped visage was inscrutable. Bin Zaid, the Captain of my Guards, I already knew by sight: he alone seemed to be simply smiling: the others wore a chilling variety of frozen grins, brilliant teeth glinting through shaggy thickets of black, grey and white.

But one, deep in a dim corner, had no exhibition of teeth on show. He looked at first like nothing but a heap of filthy old rags. In the depths of a monk-like cowl a pair of glowing eyeballs seemed the sole token of human life. I was staring in dumb alarm when suddenly he made a noise like a drain, filled his mouth with phlegm, produced a stringy grey hand from the folds and spat into its palm. The assembly sat unconcerned as he creaked groaning to his feet, tottered to the door, tossed his handful of mucus out on to my veranda and hobbled back to his nook. He withdrew into the silence of his swaddle. He now looked like a half-unravelled mummy.

After a long uncomfortable pause Sarur spoke. He began to greet me once more, but elaborately, in carefully selected terms of the most precise and courtly Arabic, falling from his lips like pearls from a cockle-shell. He welcomed me ceremoniously to Al Abr: he hoped I would enjoy my stay; and he pledged me his most cordial assistance. He flashed his teeth through his whiskers and leant back against the wall.

One by one the others took up the rigmarole. Bin Huweil's promise of help sounded like the offer of a bed for the night from Procrustes; his voice was soft and bland, dangerous as gelignite. By the way of " amen " there came a rumbling from the dirty washing in the corner. Out of the mound of rags there rose a thing like a cobra, sinuously uncoiling. It was a shrivelled grey arm, festooned with bits and pieces of garbage; the hand waved in my direction as if trying to fascinate me. I watched, fascinated indeed, while a hoarse bubbling voice pronounced its version of the litany like a Sybil prophesying doom.

Then all fell once more silent, and they looked at each other, eyebrows raised in mutual mute inquiry. I felt, knowing a little about Arabs—albeit a babe in arms among these desert men—that there was more to come.

There was.

Sarur opened the interview in earnest without further ceremony. " What are you doing about those Dahm, Assistant Adviser?" His tone was now grave, heavy with reproach that I had not already chastised his foes in the Yemen. He licked his lips with relish, took a deep breath, and launched himself into a long and obviously rehearsed speech, leaning forward from his hips where he sat. I got the impression that he had been treating every newly-arrived Political Officer to this catalogue of grievance since the Pax Britannica first dipped its toe into his land. It was a medley of bitter complaints against a heedless Government, eloquent anathemas upon a satanic Dahm, and peremptory demands that I take up the cudgels forthwith on behalf of his much-wronged Saar. " Bin Huweil " —Sarur gazed with sorrowful eyes upon a now pathetically wronged-looking Genghis Khan—" Bin Huweil went to the Dahm only last month and asked for his stolen camel back and they turned him away—turned him away, empty handed."

The well-primed Ben Huweil took up the tale in a voice now gravid with grief. His expulsion, camel-less, by the flint-hearted Dahm sounded like the story of Hagar and Ishmael, of the erring daughter turned out in the snow, of Lear on the heath. . . . Would the Assistant Adviser not do something for poor Bin Huweil? The mighty Imperial Government at his beck and call . . . his camel . . . .

" Camels." From the musty heap in the corner came another catechism. This was less emotional; more measured, controlled; a sinisterly sagacious old man, I thought. Was the Assistant Adviser wielding the sword of justice, or only the sword of the strong? Had the Assistant Adviser not the power and the force of law, armed as he was with the rifles of his soldiers—here a hand like a snake-head weaved in the direction of the fort—to uphold the rights of poor wronged old men? He too had a camel, it seemed. The camel had strayed, as camels do. But the last time he saw his camel it had been among the camels of Bin Huweil!—the grey arm subsided into the grey folds, the hoarse voice sank into its bronchial bed.

Sarur had laid a hasty hand on Bin Huweil's knee. And somebody else tactfully took up the spluttering fuse—his brother had been a Desert Guard—had served faithfully—had been unjustly dismissed—would the Assistant Adviser . . . another voice had a father who was a cripple—would the Assistant Adviser . . . the Government, long ago, had promised money for a water-tank . . . and then: when was the Assistant Adviser going to make the Saar allow free access for the Kurab tribe to Al Abr?

There was a sudden thundery hush, as if a great black cloud had swept across the sun. The assembly turned as one man to eye the last speaker. I sought the focus of their concentrated glare: I found Bin Zaid, Captain of Desert Guards. He alone was not of the Saar; he was in fact from the Kurab; and clearly he had dropped a brick. Bin Zaid gulped and stood up and made a comic mockery of a military salute and backed out of the room.

I spent the next week in full retreat—I made a tour of inspection, accompanied by Bin Zaid and a troop of the Legion. Bin Zaid filled in the background for me, free from the contentious atmosphere of that first dreadful evening. It was typical of the Saar chiefs, he told me disparagingly (gliding with ease over his own hapless contribution to the palaver). What they were doing, he wagged his head sagely as we jolted along, was making sure that I heard their version of all the current talking-points before my ears could be clogged up by a whole lot of variations from rivals in the disputes . . . the phlegmy old man in the disgusting clothes was Bogshan, he said; wealthiest, meanest, and most compulsively litigious Arab between Oman and the Yemen: a sort of Scrooge of the Sands. Owner of incalculable quantities of camels and goats, master of extravagant numbers of slaves to tend them, he passed his leisurely days spying out animals in the possession of his fellows which he hoped, by some imaginative manipulation of tribal law, to claim as his own. It was the modern equivalent of the now forbidden raid. I would be seeing a great deal more of Bogshan, said Bin Zaid with mischievous relish.

As we ground through the soft dust I began to grasp the form of this corner of my satrapy. The Hadhramaut, unique among valleys, narrows as it descends. Its mouth is only a few hundred yards wide, but at its top end, where it begins its carve through the plateau, it measures about fifty miles across. This fifty-mile throat is choked by a huge plug of sand. There is a passage through on both sides, between the dunes and the cliffs. Al Abr guards the northern route, the gateway to Saudi Arabia. The Mukalla Government maintained a customs and immigration post beneath the guns of the fort.

The sheer cliffs of the plateau stand drawn up behind Al Abr, here no longer rosy-pink but a sun-baked charcoal grey. Three eroded outcrops like Arizona mesas loom over the outpost—my first thought was " Indian Country " and I half-expected to see rows of feather-hatted braves sitting their horses on the ridge. But once out and away from the rocks the yellow desert reaches to the horizon, and to endless horizons beyond, flat as a frozen lake, a level plain of firm sand so wide and so smooth that we sped along at seventy miles an hour with the grey cliffs on our right dipping below the rim of the world.

Our first stop was Zimakh, the next well in the chain which lies like a boom along the frontier. About forty miles out from Al Abr, Bin Zaid pointed with his finger towards the distant line of cliffs. There, barely discernible, like a seagull floating far away at sea, I saw a minute white speck shimmering in the haze. The dot of white gradually grew as we raced towards it, evolving into a small white building on a little knoll. This was Zimakh fort.

As we drew near, the landscape changed. From the calm bare sands we bounced into a belt of shrubs, and beyond these rose an avenue of great green shady trees as bushy as beeches. In the wide shade of the largest we stopped, piled out, mopped our foreheads, lifted the bonnets of the bubbling Land-Rovers and unscrewed the radiator caps to let the steam subside. The soldiers brewed tea. I sat in the cool shadows and took my feet out of my shoes and wagged my toes in the breeze. Through the branches I could see the little fort, no bigger than a cottage, perched on its rock with the red and white flag of the Legion fluttering from its top. I dozed. . . .

Suddenly, we were not alone. I jerked up, feeling as if I had sat on an ant-hill, or pushed my hand into a wasps' nest. From all sides came threading through the bushes and the thorn trees little knots of white-clad figures. I heard a bleat. I looked up and there, clustered like daisies around the roots of one of the great trees, was a flock of little white goats, no bigger than cats; a black-draped shepherdess stood gazing. We had landed in the middle of a Bedouin camp. They were all round us.

I had time only to turn on Bin Zaid in dumb reproach before with something like relief I spotted Sarur; and there was Bin Huweil . . . there, too, was a new face, but clearly one of consequence, as witness the confident way he strode to the front and thrust himself forward to meet me.

This was a thick and stocky man with angry eyes and the vermilion complexion of congenital bad temper. He had a round face and a short grizzled beard, like Ernest Hemingway. His smile of welcome did nothing to ease the choleric crinkle round the eyes. His words, which were courteous enough, burst out of his mouth like a shout of fury.

Even Sarur, the supposed chieftain of this part of the world, seemed apprehensive of this irate little man. The others were positively deferential. I reflected with dismay that even the mildest of these Bedouin—even the homely chicken-clucking Bin Zaid—were by nature piratical cut-throats and blood-thirsty brigands; they killed men as readily as we write rude letters. So what was to come from a Bedouin—and one of the Al Abr Saar—who seemed to live permanently at boiling point, and to frighten even his own friends?

However, for the moment all was sweetness. Masiud, the turkey-faced man, had come to apologise for not meeting me when I arrived, and to pay his ritual respects. I invited them all to join me in a cup of coffee. We sat down in the shade and I tried to make polite conversation, wondering all the time what Masiud was going to contribute to my already bulging portfolio of Saar complaints.

He soon told me. It turned out that Masiud was also a chief of these wolves; moreover he himself thought that he was really the top chief—that Sarur was receiving the Government's wage improperly. This, though, was mentioned only in passing. I gathered that Masiud had long ago given up hope of pressing this point to a favourable conclusion; that he merely produced it on ceremonial occasions to justify his apoplectic countenance.

His real sore was a recent injustice, he said: one of his followers—" One of my children," he described him tenderly, " merely a boy, too young to know better "—had seen a stray camel passing by; had collected it and brought it to Zimakh to feed and water the poor lost creature. The camel's owners had tracked it here, but too late—Masiud's lad had sold it, to defray expenses. Ungratefully and maliciously, the pursuers had ridden straight in to the Hadhramaut to lodge a complaint. The lad, innocent of criminal intent but fearing for his life, had fled; he was now an outlaw, lurking like a hunted hare in the hills. And what was the Assistant Adviser—their only guardian against cruel Arabs and oppressive Mukalla magistrates—going to do about that?

From Zimakh I turned thankfully towards the border, to the west in the empty depths of the desert. For three blessed days of peace we hummed merrily over the level sandy plain, seeing no Arabs, hearing no grouses, meeting no belly-aching warmongers. It was bliss. And when we finally pulled up at the solitary mountain of moon-white marble which marks the frontier with the Yemen, we had a celebration feast. One of our legionary escorts had illegally and skilfully shot a gazelle, and the delectable animal was stewed with spices and consumed by us all.

There were too few such moments in the months to come.

THREE

The Judge Who Chewed the Cud

THROUGH all these early crises I trod warily, feeling my way in the fog. When the Bedouin were talking to me in cold blood they tried their best to speak an intelligible tongue; but when the heat was up they plunged back eagerly into their own dialect, an Arabic which enshrines in all its purity the language of the ancient days. It was like Chaucerian English spluttered through a rage.

I could not cry for help. I had been specifically told to keep these cataracts of tribulation off the R.A.'s desk. Such cat-fights as I had so far refereed seemed, in the climate of Al Abr, to be pregnant with earth-shattering consequences; but in the rarefied political atmosphere of Mukalla they were just like so many rooks quarrelling in a tree. I could find no clues in the crumbling piles of dust-caked files that decorated my home: for my predecessors had found it as impossible as I to maintain any coherent sort of records in this job. The best I could do was to save up the more unravellable of the tangles and carry them in to Ellis—they were none of his business, but the vast Jim was generous with his advice to a floundering novice.

My position was peculiar, and ill-defined. Properly, as " Assistant Adviser ", my post was non-administrative, non-executive. I merely " assisted " the R.A. in his own unique task of advising the Sultans. I myself was nobody's adviser; nor had I a vestige of official authority. I was, however, the only authority the Bedouin could really discern. So I had little choice but to accept the spurious mantle with which they invested me, and become a kind of Sanders of the Desert.

The tribes of the desert had enjoyed for generations a lax relationship with their Sultans, generally more formal than functional. The Kathiri Sultan claimed his own tribes who, by historical accident, acknowledged him as their ruler within certain well-marked limits and who had at some distant date signed documents of flimsy fealty. The Qaiti was in the same state; and the Sultan of Socotra had his Mahra who, when asked, admitted readily that the barbaric island chief was their sovereign, but fervently denied that he had any rights at all beyond that of rejoicing in the title.

Until the days of the pacification under Ingrams and his successors this slap-happy situation obtained throughout the desert—and indeed in most of the country, outside the cities. But slowly, through the efforts and enterprise of a series of painstaking Political Officers, one Bedouin clan after another was cajoled, corrupted or coerced into accepting a more positive dominion from its titular monarch.

Somebody now had to wield the Sultans' new sceptres, for the Sultans though happy enough to have them were reluctant to brandish them themselves in the exposed wasteland outside the walls of their city-states. So the white man took up his burden, here as elsewhere, and for many years now the more accessible tribes had been accustomed to the sight of British levies—the Legion—patrolling and garrisoning their territories, and British officials travelling amongst them and—up to a point—governing them.

The exception remained the Mahra. The shortcoming here was due to no lack of courage, nor of cunning; the campaign to subdue the Mahra had been long and hard, but it had only begun to prod at the crust. The forts of Sanau and Habarut and the relative security of the open desert around them stood as monuments to ten years of difficult and dangerous work by Jim Ellis and his colleagues. But three hurdles had always barred the way: the people's obsessive xenophobia, their Sultan's impenetrable obtuseness, and the breachless mountain barrier of their refuge.

*   *   *

Quite soon I struck an unexpected snag.

I had always understood, not without reason, that an Arab tribe has a sheikh, a chieftain with whom one can treat on behalf of his people, and through whom one can try to control them. No human community, I thought, can exist without some organisation, some palpable social structure; and moreover, sheikhs are things which Arabs have.

But not these Bedouin. The real Bedouin are men of such ineffable arrogance, such a sublime belief in their own equality under God, so porcupine-prickly an ego, that to admit anybody else's right to speak for them or title to command them is unthinkable. Bedouin can be induced to accept an imposed, extraneous authority—the soldiers of the Legion, for example, readily put on the manacles of military discipline, and the imperium of the Sultans (and even my own small sway) was never seriously in dispute. But among themselves they brook no lordship.

The two mainland Sultans had nevertheless endeavoured—with advice and encouragement—to forge a chain of command, by setting up a system of salaried sheikhs, through whom they hoped to exercise a measure of control over their free-running subjects. After a long gestation, among the Saar and Kurab and other peoples within reach of metropolitan influence, the policy was beginning to bear fruit. The tribe threw up its leaders, and the State enrolled them as civil servants. Sarur, for example, qualified by birth to be chief of his sept of the Saar, had been approved by his men but appointed by the Qaiti Government, who paid him for his pains. (It was Masiud's sincere belief that if anybody should enjoy the stipend it was he, that accounted for much of his choler). But Sarur's authority was vulnerable. It was honoured only so long as personal interest was not involved, and he had nothing but his personal prestige and character to uphold it. It could be repudiated with impunity: by his men, or indeed by himself, if it threatened to become uncomfortable. For the duties of his chieftainship were but vaguely circumscribed, and when boiled down to their essence they were two—to judge such disputes

c

as were voluntarily submitted to him, and to pay lip-service to the Sultan.

A tribe like the Saar is really one enormous family. In fact the whole of this southern race of Arabs is a family, of which the Saar are the children of one minor patriarch. The Saar split into two main sub-divisions, each named after one of the twin sons of the founder; these halves in turn are shared among the ancestor's grandchildren, and so on, proliferating down the generations until now there are as many clans and septs within the tribe as holes in a sponge. One might thus expect the tribe to run like a huge orderly household, with the father ruling his children, the head of the family lording it over his relatives and being in turn subject to the next senior pater-familias, right up the ladder to the top.

But this would be too much organisation for the desert men. The Saar have a multitude of small chiefs like Sarur, paid by the Sultan for keeping their own houses in order, and they have two Chief Justices—one for each half of the tribe—whose jurisdiction is supreme. The system gains in simplicity what it loses in formal precision. Granted goodwill on all sides, a dispute is settled by the local Sarur; he apportions blame, allots compensation; if his decision is contested, the case is taken up to the appropriate Chief Justice. One of these is senior to the other, and can hear appeals from his colleague, but beyond this august level further appeal is almost impossible. This, however, stipulates goodwill on all sides. There is no backbone of effective authority—neither to enforce compliance with a judgement, nor even to compel attendance at the bar.

And there was the rub.

When I had investigated the apparent facts concerning Masiud's hot-headed youngster, in the case which Masiud himself had forced upon my attention at Zimakh, and I had ascertained that the lad was no more than a runaway camel thief whom it was my manifest duty to pursue, I got my first taste of Bedouin organisation and method.

The boy—Rikaiz was his name—had fled into the enveloping obscurity of the Arabian desert. Masiud alone, so far as I knew, could find him. I might despatch whole regiments of the Legion to scour the sands: they would search for seven years in vain. All I could do was demand his body from that smouldering ball of wrath who was supposed to be his immediate family chief.

I may as well have addressed myself to Masiud's camel. Masiud stood mendaciously, but obdurately, ignorant of Rikaiz's hideout. The fact that Masiud received no salary certainly weakened my arm—why should he help, after all? —but when I approached Sarur, as the official chief, I was no happier. Sarur, he politely told me, was no policeman. Sarur was judge of his clan, no more. If a dispute, and the disputants, were brought before him, Sarur would judge: according to the customs of the tribe and the laws of God. But Sarur had a family. He had goats, and he had camels. He could not leap off into the wilderness in search of fugitive malefactors, however bad. And this, of course, was not the point at all.

So I travelled to the court of the paramount judge of this half of the Saar. Surely, I thought, one stern command from the lips of the great man would bring Rikaiz running—or at least his head on a charger.

The Chief Justice lived on the plateau. A tortuous handmade path writhed its way up a cliff behind Zimakh and led drearily across a hard grey upland towards a cluster of drystone buildings and square brown towers like small Scottish brochs, which looked as if they were sliding down a slope into a ravine. The judge's chambers were not what I had expected of a desert chief. I had been dreaming vaguely of brocaded tents, rich pavilions, Negro bodyguards with sabre on thigh. This one occupied a complex of dilapidated barns where the division between living-quarters, sheep-byre, and straw loft was as blurred as in an Irish cottage. But here was the ultimate seat of justice. Bin Jerboa was my last hope.

Which particular ancestor of this extraordinary magistrate can have resembled a desert jumping rat? The " Bin " of these names refers more often to some remote and mythical forebear than to the man's own father. The judges of the Saar had been " Sons of the Jerboa " for as long as anybody could remember.

But there was something about the current holder of the title that fitted the name. He was very old: he looked like a troll, or a gnome. He had spindly legs and the feet of a chimpanzee and gnarled knuckly hands. He came bobbing out of his stone hut to greet me, stooped like a rheumatic Merlin, the weight of his huge head seeming too great for his shoulders. He opened his mouth and showed me one or two long jagged fangs. In the corner of his lower lip lay an interesting bulge like a boil, which he sucked with obvious enjoyment. Nodding his head as big as a barrel he led me into his castle.

The Bedouin do not usually live in any sort of building. These hovels—virtually hollow cairns—are communal property, defensive citadels, of the Saar. Only the judge, Bin Jerboa, enjoying a state of advanced decrepitude, spent most of his time in their dim nooks. The place was squalid, but with nothing of the sordid filth of a European slum: it was more like a decently kept stable or kennel. The floor was strewn with coarse rush mats and goat droppings and slumbering Arabs. The loose stone walls were black with generations of charcoal smoke, filmy with a myriad spider-webs. There was very little else, pleasant or unpleasant.

I sat down cross-legged and awaited with apprehensive stomach the dreaded but inexorable meal. The arrival of the Assistant Adviser necessitated the killing of a goat. It arrived after three or four hours: a mountain of soggily stewed rice with a dismembered billy, bleakly boiled, arranged around the sad white heap. The advent of this unsavoury dish was the signal for the gathering of the clans. From all sides—from smoke-dark crannies in the barn, from noisome blankets on the floor, from the warren of hovels outside, there rapidly assembled a ravenous pack of wolves in men's clothing. They shuffled up to squat slavering around the dreadful feast and delved with great horny fists into the pile of fodder and crammed it by the handful into their mouths. Bedouin are like wild dogs. Never knowing whence or when their next meal will come—though Allah is good—they stuff themselves like Strasbourg geese whenever they find food before them, and will starve in cheerful resignation for the next month with nothing to eat but a daily handful of millet-grain or some camel-milk cheese-rind. Here at Host Jerboa's the Arabs made pigs of themselves, unashamedly and with joy.

I couldn't eat a thing. But I had naturally fed that morning and I would eat again next day. My table-companions had no such assurance. They gorged.

Among the guests at Jerboa's Feast was a well-dressed man who had come, I learnt from my neighbour at the rice, from the Yemen. A well-dressed Bedouin is one whose clothes are clean: this one sported a shiny yellow gown, with a brightly-coloured cloth wrapped around his head. He was a plaintiff at Jerboa's bench. One of the Saar was defendant, and following the rules the complainant was prosecuting his suit at the tribal court of his adversary.

The fact that all—plaintiff, defendant, judge, and jury—were alike amicably stuffing their faces with fistfuls of meat around the same dish was merely the way things are done in the desert. Anyone who proposes to eat becomes automatically host to everybody within nostril range of his pot. Equally, anyone feeling the rumblings of appetite need seek no further than the nearest column of woodsmoke.

After the last gristly handful had been wiped into the last greasy mouth, and the last rice-garnished hand was washed in the tin pot of water—which by now looked like a tureen of Irish stew, the Court assembled. Bin Jerboa revealed the secret of what he sucked in the corner of his mouth. He fished out a handful of ground tobacco from a nasty corner of his clothing, mixed it with some white ash from the fire and rolled it between his thumb-balls to make a plum-sized gobstopper. Opening his mouth—it was like the entrance to a cavern, with stalagmites and stalactites dripping in the dank murk—he placed the gobbet with precise care between his lower right molars and his nether lip. For the remainder of the proceedings he sucked his disgusting bonbon with sensuous relish.

On Bin Jerboa's right sat the Yemen man. On his left was the defendant. I was not surprised at all to see that this was Masiud, purple with righteous wrath. The Yemeni was calm:

he clearly thought himself more than a cut above these savage
Saar. The rest of the circle, apart from myself—and I was in
grave danger of forgetting the purpose of my visit—composed
a kind of accidental jury. They were simply Saar who had happened to be passing by, had sniffed Jerboa's goat from afar,
and had ambled up to take what God had set in their way.
Now sated, they would post-prandially take part in the judicial
inquiry ahead.

There is nothing a Bedouin loves more than a nice piece of
itigation. It is like Pavlova's Swan to a balletomaine : the Derby
to punters : the latest singer to adolescent girls. It is, apart
from raiding and coition, their only earthly pleasure. But these
were not a jury in any decisive sense. It would scarcely be fair
for a complainant, seeking justice from his enemy's chief, to
have his case subjected to a jury of the defendant's clansmen.
And Bedouin justice is, above all things, rigorously equitable.
The casual assembly could comment, knowledgeably or not,
upon the technical nuances of the case—and Bedouin justice,
though unwritten, is exhaustively codified; they could recall
precedents to the infirm mind of an aged judge; they could
discuss among themselves the legal principles involved, as an
enjoyable abstract exercise. But the decision lay with the
judge. In this case, it lay with Bin Jerboa, sitting Buddha-
legged and apparently asleep with the globule of tobacco in his
mouth while the man from the Yemen expatiated on his woes.

I had great difficulty in following the archaic Arabic, compounded as it was with the terminology of a jurisprudence that
ante-dates Islam by a thousand years. But I got the drift. The
Yemeni had purchased a camel from a neighbour, paying
sound money for it (" my own money," he was careful to point
out). Some time later Masiud had noticed this camel watering
at Al Abr, and had known it for one of his own, which had
disappeared a few months before.

Masiud had seized the beast; and Masiud had it still.

The Yemeni said it was his camel: he had bought it. Masiud
said it was his: it had been stolen from him.

Bin Jerboa chewed his wad, and the jury chewed the facts.
For among the Bedouin, where everybody knows everybody

over a land the size of Europe, fact is never in dispute at law. The only question to be decided was, who should have the camel?

In civilised law, to be sure, stolen property belongs to its original owner, and its current possessor—no matter how innocently he obtained it—has no title at all. But Bedouin law is different. Bedouin law must recognise a society where looting camels is a customary sport, the principal daylight recreation of the people. Taking a camel in the course of a raid is perfectly fair: all the deprived owner can do is to go and take somebody else's.

But raids are raids, and plain thievery in the night is something quite distinct. And Masiud averred, with explosive emphasis, that his camel had been *stolen*—the clear division between " larceny " and " plunder " is embalmed in the Arabic tongue to this day. So the Yemen man's plea must fail, said Masiud.

The Yemeni came back with a quiet rebuttal. His purchase of the camel had been transacted in complete ignorance of the beast's antecedents, and therefore, in equity, his deal was valid. Had he known the animal was stolen, then of course Masiud would have had a point; but as things stood, Masiud should seek the thief and exact retribution from him, not from the innocent Yemeni.

Slowly, almost imperceptibly—like a silent crowd beginning, one by one, to murmur—the jury of Jerboa's guests joined in the combat. After a few minutes the dim smoke-black room was a confusion of twittering, jabber, and growl, with here and there a more forceful voice brushing the others aside with a contemptuous asseveration of fact. Only the judge sat silent, masticating his gross cud. The Yemeni spread out his hands, smiling condescendingly, explaining points of law to the yammering Saar with long-suffering reasonableness. Masiud stewed in his place, growing redder and redder and angrier and angrier, his speech a succession of querulous quacks.

Choosing his moment with care, just before Masiud seemed likely to burst into flame and the meeting to erupt into riot, Bin Jerboa made a decisive move. He thrust out his lower lip like an anthropoid ape, carefully—as if extracting a loose tooth—inserted two of his knotted fingers, and lifted out the soggy mass of tobacco and ash and laid it on the fire beside him. It sizzled.

The gathering hushed, leaving only Masiud blaring like a solo trumpet—then he too realised that the moment of judgement had come, and he fell silent, steaming.

Bin Jerboa cleared his throat of some glutinous obstruction and in a voice as old and as wise as the crabbed Merlin he was, pronounced a judgement that Solomon would have admired.

The Yemeni, said he, must relinquish his claim to the camel forthwith: for the camel was Masiud's. I watched Masiud settle back on his haunches and smile, as Shylock smiled at the opening of Portia's speech. But . . . Masiud's smile abandoned his eyes, though it still stretched his mouth—the Yemeni had bought the camel in good faith, so Masiud must refund him the price. Masiud—Jerboa held up a hand to silence his now outraged tribesman—Masiud must file another suit, against the thief, if and when he discovered him, to recover his money. For Masiud's oppressor was he, not the man from the Yemen.

The case was closed. I saw somebody scribbling with a battered fountain-pen on a scrap of paper which he held in the palm of his hand. This was Jerboa's clerk—the old man was as illiterate as a camel. The clerk handed his fragment to Bin Jerboa, who clasped the pen in his fist and scratched a spidery squiggle across the bottom.

The judgement was signed. All that remained was for the clerk to make two more copies, one for the Yemeni and one for Masiud, which neither could read but which would be produced for interpretation in the event of appeal. Each tucked his precious charter into the wallet on his cartridge belt, already stuffed with a quantity of previous judgements rolled tightly into minute balls.

The party broke up. Only I stayed on with Bin Jerboa, for I had business of my own. I now had small hope that the sage would urge Masiud to disgorge Rikaiz; for one thing, Masiud was in no mood to be touched on the subject; for another, Bin Jerboa would be tactfully at pains to avoid exasperating the angry man any further. However, I had my duty, and I plunged in. Would the judge, I asked with ponderous deference, issue an injunction to Masiud to deliver the criminal he was harbouring to the justice of the Government?

Bin Jerboa champed.

" No," he said.

I had to wait while he performed the leisurely ritual of composing another wad for his mouth. When it was safely in place, looking like the most frightful toothache, Bin Jerboa bent upon me the kindly gaze of a grown-up to an innocent child and said that it was not his job. The Government was all-powerful, he said, or it damn well ought to be with all its soldiers; I had my Desert Guards; I must find the man. When brought before him, said Bin Jerboa, Rikaiz would face the utmost rigour of the law. But Bin Jerboa was a judge: he was not a king.

And there the matter rested.

For the remainder of my tour in the desert I was dogged, faithfully and persistently, by three men, who waylaid me whenever they could and whom I used every ruse to avoid. One was the Mukalla Government man who asked me, every time he succeeded in crossing my path, when I was going to do my job and bring Rikaiz to court. One was the Yemeni, whom I saw less often but with no less dismay, who asked me when I was going to do my job and get Masiud to pay up. And the third was Masiud, the most importunate of all, living as he did on my doorstep. Masiud had been wronged, said Masiud. It was all the Government's fault. In the old days he would have launched a raid, seized a camel, sold it and paid the cash he owed the Yemeni. Now the Government would not allow it. So, said Masiud, the Government must bear the consequences of its policy. I must give Masiud the cash; then he would discharge his debt; and the Yemeni and he, and I, would thereafter be everlasting friends.

I thought I would be clever. I had funds, in limited quantity, which were at my disposal for use in worthy causes such as keeping the desert quiet. I told Masiud that I would pay his debt—if he surrendered Rikaiz. By one master *coup*, I hoped, I would let slip three millstones from around my neck.

But I had misjudged my man—indeed I had misunderstood the whole Bedouin code of chivalry, which is stricter than anything Arthur and Lancelot knew.

Masiud narrowed his eyes, and I felt myself the living personification of Perfidious Albion. For if Rikaiz had been a real criminal, a transgressor against the Bedouin concept of good and bad, Masiud would not have succoured him for an hour. If he had disgraced himself, so he had disgraced Masiud's clan, and the Saar as a whole. I would have had him for the asking. But Rikaiz had done no such thing. He had raided over the border: in retaliation for some foray the Saudi tribe had made—perhaps a month before, perhaps twenty years ago; it was no matter. The fact was that Rikaiz had acted within the bounds of decency. The pious injunctions of the Government —British and Qaiti—that raiding should cease might have brought calm to the area but they had done nothing to change the Bedouin's views on what was right and what was wrong.

Masiud would more willingly go to prison himself than betray his man; and the gaol to a Bedouin is preferable only to death.

In my despair I sought refuge in the reflection that the Saar were, after all, but one tribe, and that my diocese encompassed at least four others, not even counting the Mahra: that the Al Abr parish was but a fifth of the whole: that I could easily, and justifiably, escape the lot and enjoy a prolonged holiday visiting my other parishioners. The thought that I might be leaping from the frying pan into the fire did not rise up to worry me at the time.

I saddled my Land-Rover, summoned my cook, and took off for the far north.

FOUR

"Monarch of All I Survey"

PLUMB in the middle of my 50-miles-to-the-inch map lay a small round dot labelled Thamud. This place can be found on many a chart of southern Arabia, masquerading as a fair-sized provincial town. Indeed, Thamud is the metropolis of the Northern Deserts, so I gathered from my dusty files. At any rate there was one great attraction, for me: there seemed to be no Saar at Thamud at all, only some mild-sounding people called Manahil and Awamer.

The fact that I was really fleeing to the depths of the desert from the nightmare lawsuits of the Saar weighed light on my conscience. I had plenty to do up there: chiefs to meet; Guards to pay; three garrisons to inspect; sixty thousand square miles to explore. My map showed me two routes to Thamud, one of three hundred miles involving an alarming amount of sand dunes, and the other about two hundred miles over the wind-swept plateau. I chose the latter, as seeming obviously preferable, ignoring the passionate protests of my driver.

My Land-Rover was home for the next three weeks. I sat in the front, with my feet up on the dashboard braced against the bumps. Beside me was Faraj the driver, who knew the way though he patently hated it; Faraj was a lean and blue-black legionary of Nubian antecedents. The back of the vehicle was well stuffed with bedding rolls, boxes of food (mostly rice and tinned tunny and tea), an ammunition box of kitchenware (mostly enamelled tin plates and Primus stoves), a dozen of

Scotch, and Hassan my cook. Hassan reclined like a dining Roman upon the bedding rolls, and as I looked at him I shuddered—for not the first time. He was a weedy Hadhramaut youth with a thin yellow face and goofy rabbit teeth. He wore the clothes of the Hadhramaut: a grimy shirt flapping over an elegant ankle-length sarong of floral blue cotton, as inappropriate in this man's desert as a straw hat and flannels. Hassan was to prove his worth, and more, but at the beginning of my trek I could only shrug my shoulders and reflect that he was the best cook I had. To make a Bedouin into a servant is impossible: no man was ever their master, nor do they regard work as a decent way for any man (except a slave) to pass his time. So the Hadhramaut was the only place I could recruit. And Hassan was the only volunteer. To the elegant citizens of the valley, the desert is a horrid place like St. Antony's wilderness, peopled by red-eyed wolves and savages who cut throats for fun. Hassan, for all his discouraging appearance, had a strange lust for adventure, and he came; and he stayed with me throughout.

Bumping along behind was a vehicle called my pick-up, a sort of small lorry containing five 44-gallon drums of petrol and water and nothing else. Every time we dipped into a gully or clambered over a boulder—the deceptively level plateau road was soon making me doubt the wisdom of my choice —a moment or so later came a thunderous clang as of gates of brass: the pick-up's load of drums were tightly lashed with rope but still they leaped and pounded like Tubal's hammer within their bonds. For the thing was designed on a curious principle. Land-Rovers have four-wheel drive, but the pick-up was merely a truck, with drive to the rear wheels only. To compensate for this handicap its makers had installed a Goliath of a six-cylinder engine powerful enough to propel a tank, and springs like a railway wagon's. Unable to grind its way through sand and dust, like the Land-Rover, this bull of a lorry merely snorted, gathered itself, and charged. Some of the gullies were rutted with ridges of sand a yard high: the truck, galloping up at thirty miles an hour, would leap bodily over the whole gully in a series of exuberant hops

like a steeplechaser. The driver, a robust Saar youth named
Saleh, was used to this kind of progress. I tried riding in
the pick-up for a mile or two, and emerged green-faced,
bruised, and twitching. Saleh had a thousand miles ahead of
him.

My little convoy of two had clambered up the winding pathway that leads to Jerboa's castle, and now we drove away
to the north across the stony table-land. The road rapidly
degenerated into a broad ribbon of wheel-ruts; sometimes we
were ploughing through a thick slush of white dust which filled
the cab and choked our eyes and ears and nostrils, sometimes
rasping over glass-sharp flints and slaty flakes of limestone
which ripped and slashed at the tyres. We rode a razor-back
between great scooped-out ravines, we wound serpent-like
among an interminable range of flat-topped hills. We saw not
a living thing, except here and there a tuft of thorny grass, and
occasionally a baked-looking lizard. The whole petrified world
was the colour of sun-dried mud. It was hideous; and the
words of Cowper repeated themselves over and over in my
head as we ground and jolted along :

> I am monarch of all I survey,
> My right there is none to dispute . . .
> Oh solitude, where are the charms
> That sages have seen in thy face?
> Better dwell in the midst of alarms
> Than reign in this horrible place.

And the bucketing pick-up's anvil-clangs punctuated the verse,
as the table-top knolls passed one by one and I felt adrift on
a shoreless sea of stone.

At midday we stopped at the first cluster of breast-high
bushes, dry as tinder but offering some meagre shade. Hassan
tumbled out of his sleep in the back, heaved out boxes and
began to cook me some rice with a tin of tunny slopped into it.
The drivers mended two flat tyres and wandered off to brew
tea. I levered myself out of my seat, stretched my creaking
joints, blew the dust out of my mouth and nose, rubbed my
numb buttocks, and collapsed back on the seat again. Soon

Hassan brought me a pinky-grey mess on a tin plate and I had lunch where I sat, while the Arabs squatted under a shrub and dunked chapattis into their tea.

Then we were off again.

I am monarch of all I survey . . .

By evening, with two more punctures to our credit, we had reached half-way to Thamud. Here we saw our first animal life of a higher order than lizards: a lone camel; followed shortly by a mahogany-coloured man with a blue cloth wrapped round him like a scanty toga. He hailed us; we stopped. He came sprinting up as though his house was on fire. He carried a rifle in a fringed gazelle-skin case, and wagged it menacingly as he ran, but when he stopped at my door he seemed affable enough.

" What's the news?" he bellowed through the window, in a voice like a football fan. His face was about two inches from my ear, and I flinched at the blast.

" Peace," I tried. Later I learnt to shout back at these northern Bedouin as vehemently as they yelled at me. They are incapable of talking in a normal conversational voice, they always treat their listener as if he is half a mile away.

" Where from?" he roared.

" Al Abr," I screamed.

" Where to?"—" Thamud."

" Water."

He suddenly thrust out a thing like a mummified cat; Faraj leant across me and took it without a word and filled it with a rubber tube, syphon-fashion, from a jerrican. Faraj was an old desert traveller.

The water-skin, now bloated and dripping like a drowned cat, was snatched back by the stranger who shoved his face into mine and hollered: " Go in peace!"

By now thoroughly unnerved I signalled Faraj to drive on, and as I looked back I saw the Arab waving his hairy rifle in salute. Faraj told me then that if we hadn't stopped, the fellow would have shot at us: with no malice, merely to emphasise his right to accost us in his home territory, and to ask us for news, and to recharge his water-skin. I never made the experiment—I took Faraj's word for it, and most of my desert journeys were enlivened by such incidents, *fortissimo* but amicable.

We stopped for the night in a bare and forsaken stretch of the stone sea and as soon as the sun went down the wind came up, howling from Siberian snow-fields and chilling me stiff. Hassan set up a camp chair and table and I sat there, feeling rather like a statue of Memnon, until the glacial gale forced me to huddle in a blanket over a tin mug of whisky. It fell quickly dark, and faithful Hassan brought me a hurricane lamp and shuffled back to make my supper. The drivers were cosily cooking theirs already, over a tempting fire. I might have joined them; but I suddenly longed to be alone, with my whisky and my memories of Trafalgar Square. I supposed morosely that experienced desert travellers bring astrakhan greatcoats. I drank and shivered; and when Hassan appeared again, this time with the dreaded grey-pink platter, I spooned a few dolorous mouthfuls and crawled into my camp bed and stared disenchanted at the stars.

Morning, however, was glorious. The sunrise warmed me awake; next stop Thamud, Metropolis of the North.

This day was a replica of the last, except that the land grew gradually less bleak, the melancholy mesas died away behind us, and here and there we crossed belts of bushes and broad sandy watercourses. The terrain now was gentler, the colour rosier, the going softer: my pick-up was bounding along behind us like a demented kangaroo, drums clashing like cymbals.

As evening drew in and the sky went violet, there before us far away I discerned, as at Zimakh, a tiny white speck shimmering on a vast gravelly plain. Around it was a peppering of little bushes, looking almost lush after our barren journey.

The fort of Thamud expanded slowly into a square white building flying the red and white flag of the Legion. As we came near I heard a plaintive bugle-call, and the flag climbed down its pole. I saw soldiers presenting arms. I was home again.

This military cube is not, however, the Thamud of the maps. The real Metropolis of the North lies outside, about fifty yards away. It is a hole in the ground. Clustered around it that evening were eighty or a hundred camels, grunting and slobbering, jostling and defecating, while near-naked Arabs heaved up water in great skin bags to the tune of a monotonous chant. These men wore indigo-blue cloths around their loins and nothing else. They were dark-visaged, lean of shank, wild-looking. Compared with my white-clad courteous Saar, they seemed animals. Were these, I thought with a pang of dismay, the Manahil and the Awamer?

Thamud well is so ancient that it now lies in a small hill, volcano-like, a miniature Fujiyama composed of uncountable bowel-loads of compacted camel dung. Every generation or so the top must be built up to keep it out of the remorselessly rising mound of manure. This well is about forty feet deep, modest for the country—Zimakh, for example, goes down to more than two hundred feet, and there are others on the same scale. The stone blocks lining these venerable shafts are scored and gouged into grooves, inches deep, running all the way down to the water; the ropes of centuries have eaten into the rock so that now they run up and down in convenient channels.

I gazed in awe at this monument. Here, a fortnight's march from the nearest habitable land, some prehistoric wanderer had decided to sink a well—through bone-hard limestone. For what mad reason, with what occult guidance (only a few miles from Thamud, water has not been found at many hundreds of feet), with what Stone Age tools—I could not guess. And how to account for Zimakh, hewn through thirty-five fathoms of rock by people so remote that they are not even legendary? The Bedouin have no clue—the holes are simply there; without them, the Bedouin would not be there either. It is a chicken-and-egg enigma.

Thamud is the name of a people recorded in the Koran, to

whom the prophet Saleh brought the word of God seven generations before Abraham left Ur of the Chaldees. Perhaps in those days the desert was clothed in green, and these harsh hills of stone were rolling downs; water lay close to the surface, easily tapped; but as the ages passed the climate changed, the rain ceased, the grass dried up and the water sunk lower and lower into the limestone beds. So perhaps the people found themselves obliged continually to dig, chasing the vital stuff down as it retreated into the earth.

The road to Thamud is lined with mystifying relics, long avenues of neatly placed triliths, some with incised inscriptions in a forgotten language—no relation to the Himyaritic runes of the Hadhramaut. Nobody knows who set up these careful landmarks, or when, or why. They stand today as cenotaphs of a lost race. All that remains is the great well, and a name on the map, and a myth in the Koran.

When Jim Ellis first came to Thamud in 1953 he found it merely a muddy pit on top of the mound, half-filled with filth; here and there a dark indigo figure lurked in the surrounding rocks. The Bedouin who passed that way, only half a generation ago, must lie up and scout, making sure that no hostile band is watering there; then they approach the precious place with caution, leaving sentries to cover them while they dig out the well and fill their skins and slake their camels' thirst. In all probability they then shovel soil and muck back into the shaft, to delay pursuit. With the arrival of Ellis and the Legion, and the building of the fort, those days are past for ever and Thamud has become an oasis of comparative peace. It is in such places, and among such people, that British Imperialism is accounted a blessing, and its agents regarded as benefactors.

I spent the night in the " rest house ", a small upper room of the fort with attached kitchen. There was no inside latrine; the soldiers, like the Bedouin, fertilised the bushes around the fort, and although some fastidious precursor of mine had recently erected a small outbuilding with a hole in the floor for the use of visiting gentry, I was by now well used to the idea

D

that I had all Arabia for my lavatory, and I too chose my bush. The only obstacle to my abdominal ease was the guard, who punctiliously turned out and presented arms to me whenever I emerged: a courtesy which I found flattering but inconvenient, as the water at Thamud is spectacularly aperient and on my first morning, before I was inured to its explosive effect, I was in some haste to find a bush.

Hassan had meanwhile established himself like Escoffier in the kitchen and was preparing rice; and soon I met my first Manahil tribesman.

He took pride in his name of Tomatum, which is Arabic for tomato. His father's name had been Harbi, which means bellicose. Tomato son of Warlike was a man as remarkable as his title. He had been in the old days a kind of Ulysses, renowned far beyond the frontiers of the Manahil for his preternatural cunning and unlimited resourcefulness, priceless attributes in the permanent state of war in which the tribe then lived. No raid was complete without the son of Warlike; every party of marauders planning a descent upon the Yemen, the Kurab or the hard-pressed Mahra sought Tomatum's strategic flair and reassuring presence. When Jim Ellis burst in upon Thamud with his gospel of Law and Order for the North, Tomatum prudently turned game-keeper and volunteered his services. So invaluable had he become, so indispensable a counsellor to a succession of desperate Assistant Advisers, that he was now on the payroll of Her Majesty's Government as general Poo Bah in Thamud.

Tomatum lived in a small stone hut a hundred yards from the fort, where he passed his idle hours indulging his hobby of breeding Manahil. He had made, I think, twelve little Manahil by the time I first met him. The fifth, symbolising Tomatum's break with the days of yore, was named Jerrican.

Tomatum strolled into my room in the fort that first morning, without ceremony, greeted me as if he saw me every day of his life, and sat down on the floor. He was nothing like the Al Abr men. He was small and neat, with an almost beardless face, dark and sharp as a monkey. He wore a rainbow-coloured cloth round his waist, a fairly clean singlet, and a brilliant scarf draped over his shoulder like a Highlander's plaid. He hitched his plaid, scratched his crutch, held out his hand for a cigarette and began to tell me all about Thamud.

By the time he had finished I was wishing myself snugly back at Al Abr among the comparatively tractable Saar. For at Thamud, I learnt, there was no recognisable structure of clan chiefs and tribal judges, to whom the petty daily business could be referred. The Manahil and their enemies, the Awamer, owned chiefs of a kind, men who had been formidable leaders of the raid in their day; but they were now in virtual retirement, in receipt of pittances from the Sultans, the Manahil from the Qaiti and the Awamer from the Kathiri—personifying the permanent but dormant Problem of Thamud, which was claimed by both tribes and both Sultans, with the Mahra and their crazy king chiming in regularly to say the place was really theirs. (Thamud belonged, in the pre-Ellis days, to whichever tribe happened to be there at the time. It was an ironical paradox of history that the British Peace had in many places, such as here, brought abscesses to a head where beforehand they had been merely chronic cases of bad blood.)

So the chiefs of these men were of small use to me. They lived far from Thamud, in the Hadhramaut tributaries; it took weeks to locate them; nor were they in the least concerned with the maintenance of tribal discipline. I must deal with this myself, with the Garrison Commander despatching the day-to-day trivia in my absence. There was one compensation. Thamud was so nodal a watering place, and so remote from its nearest neighbour, that often all the arm of the law had to do was rest and wait until a wanted man, or at least his camel, came sooner or later to the well: weeks, even months, mean little in the desert.

With the eagerly offered aid of Tomato son of Warlike, I was to judge at Thamud on my own.

FIVE

Flints and Gypsum

SANAU, I had been warned, was the foulest place on earth. Skulking amid bitter white gypsum hills, that gleamed ghostly in the moonlight and glared with leprous pallor by day, the well of Sanau was a loathsome pit of sulphurous slime that stank for thirty miles around. Sanau lay in the heart of the Mahra, infested by the most unmanageable creatures that ever slunk on two legs. Sanau was also a favourite spa for the Rashid, a tribe of Arabs from the depths of the Empty Quarter who detested the Mahra with every fibre of their being, and whom the Mahra regarded as cat regards dog.

Sanau, I thought, was going to be hell.

We were travelling on again, myself, Hassan, Faraj and Saleh. A hundred miles away—going always north and east—was the next fort. Sanau. Human existence at this vile spot depended now upon a deep bore pump, drilled four hundred feet into the gypsum rock by the oil company before they lost their illusions about the Hadhramaut. The old stink-hole had recently collapsed, anyway; so if the pump broke down there would be huge disaster. The pump was always giving trouble, I had gathered. Mahra and Rashid were always at each other's throats. The place stank to heaven; and it would drive me insane.

Such were my meditations as I caught the first whiff of Sanau long before the horrible white hills came in sight. It reminded me of rotten eggs simulated in school laboratories—

sulphuretted hydrogen came irresistibly to mind. The stench was not, in fact, the well itself. The water of Sanau has so volcanic an effect on the bowels of man and beast that even camels, long inured to filthy and cathartic drink, leave a trail of fœtid stools for two or three days' march after partaking of the rare liquor. It was this nasty spoor that I was now following, with pinched nostrils, as we drove through a stark moon-like countryside. By the time the expected white speck appeared, in its bowl of death-coloured hills, I was beginning to understand what my helpful advisers had been talking about. As evening fell and we finally pulled to a halt before the sad little block-house my morale was running out at my heels.

The twilit plains surrounding the fort were a milling throng of great black beasts like a prairie-full of buffalo. Winding in over the hills from every direction were more and more, long strings of camels coming in from the far wastes of sand to fill up for the next fortnight. Little knots of frightening men sat around crackling fires, beetle-browed, long-fanged, withdrawn. I was now used to Arabs, and was no more than mildly alarmed by them *en masse*, so long as they were not actively on the warpath. But these silent savages, some with their hair in oily shoulder-length plaits like clusters of greased cord, some with rawhide thongs round scalps of tufted bristle, were clearly no Arabs. They were Mahra: and they were worse than I had feared.

As the eructating herds of camels accumulated, as the bands of neolithic-looking men loped thirstily in, I saw on a hill a neat camp of fine black tents, with here and there a tall dignified figure erect, like Moses, in a shining white robe and a long regal head-cloth—the Rashid, the Lordly Ones of Arabia, keeping antiseptically apart from the beastly Mahra.

I thought of the twenty soldiers in their tiny fort, I thought of myself, by now seven hundred miles from Mukalla. I heard a gentle chugging from a little engine, which looked as innocently incongruous as I felt in this wild chaos, and I thought of the four hundred feet of narrow pipe in which nothing must go wrong—at least until the well diggers finished mending the filthy hole in the ground.

These saviours were a jolly band of Hadhramaut artisans,
sent up by Jim Ellis before I left Mukalla. What they thought
of life out here on the edge of the world I never asked, but I
admired their courage, for the townsman of the Hadhramaut
looks on even Al Abr as a vestibule of Gehenna, even the gentle
Saar—for whom I was feeling increasingly homesick—as the
fellest of assassins.

But the blessed pump kept pumping, this time; and the
balloon-bellied camels were filled; and the Rashid kept to their
hill, and the Mahra squatted glowering, but minding their own
business on the pallid plain; and I had nothing to worry about,
but my own colon's reaction to the water . . . and Sulayim bin
Domaish.

I had been warned, too, about Sulayim bin Domaish. He
was a kind of unregenerated Tomatum; that is to say, he was
as wily, as unscrupulous, as ambitious and ubiquitous as the
Ulysses of Thamud, but he was not even nominally on our
side. He was the biggest single nuisance-factor in the whole
Northern Desert, from Oman to the Yemen; he needed an
Assistant Adviser all to himself; wherever one saw Sulayim, at
Sanau, Al Abr, or even Mukalla—for he was a man of the
world—there was trouble; and wherever there was trouble,
Sulayim was lurking close at hand.

When he came to see me in the fort to pay his respects I
was aware, first, of a gargantuan nose, which seemed to fill
the small square room. Below this grotesque Fagin-beak was
a prissily-pursed mouth, prim as a choirboy saying " prunes "
but wryly askew. Above this schnozzle sat two black eyeballs, moist and opaque as pickled walnuts. If he had walked
on to the stage of a Victorian melodrama he would have been
hissed straight through the back-drop. He was so unabashedly
evil, so extravagantly villainous, that I thought of Iago, of
Councillor Lindorf, of Mephistopheles. . . .

He settled himself down with comfortable dignity, pulled
out of somewhere in his brimstone-coloured gown a cartridge-
case open at both ends, took a small skin bag from the dark
Kashmir shawl around his head, filled the brass tube with
tobacco and politely asked me for a match. When this Plutonic

cigarette was alight he smiled at me—I thought of Gorgons, of basilisks, of cockatrices—and then, like Tomatum at Thamud, he introduced me to Sanau.

Sanau, said Sulayim, in a low Svengali voice, speaking Arabic with a broth-thick accent and worse grammar than mine—Sanau was the property of the Mahra. The Rashid were trespassers; the Rashid should be expelled. For an hour Sulayim bin Domaish explained the iniquities perpetrated upon the Mahra by my simple predecessors who did not understand, the sufferings the Mahra had borne with patience while foreign barbarians like the Rashid stole their water and their grazing under the guns of the new fort . . . but the patience of the Mahra was not inexhaustible—the Mahra looked to me, their friend, to secure their just rights, because the gentle Mahra were ever reluctant to take up arms, but unless . . . and Sulayim, he said, was the acknowledged spokesman of all the Mahra, their recognised intercessor; with Sulayim at my side I would find my path made smooth; without Sulayim . . . beneath the whole long bland discourse ran an ice-cold undercurrent of menace.

At the end of the interview Sulayim stood up, gave me another smile which turned my spine to an icicle, and stalked with serpentine grace out of the fort and away.

Habarut is the end of the road. A hundred and ninety miles from Sanau, after two dead days of rolling gravel desert and wide rivers of talc-soft sand, where the only fellow creature was a solitary buzzard circling over the rustling skeletal shrubs, Habarut was a Garden of Eden. Here, on the frontier with the Sultanate of Muscat and Oman, the last fort stood, on a bluff overlooking a valley where water—sweet soft water—flowed constantly among thickets of tall rushes and clusters of wild palms and shrubberies of oleander. I took my first bath for twelve days, luxuriating in water like nectar after the harsh gut-scouring fluid of Thamud and Sanau. Only the thought of the six hundred miles back to Al Abr marred my happy lassitude.

For Habarut seemed a paradise. I could see no problems:

no Sulayim, no camels, no quarrels; in fact, there was not a Bedouin in sight. It was an interlude of delicious peace, in an oasis of verdure, where I had nothing to do but soak and sleep.

I hardly listened, a dreamy smile relaxing my face, while the fort commander strove to impress upon me that Habarut, too, had its dark side: that Habarut, in plain fact, was probably the knottiest place of all, its people the most obstinate, its quarrels the most insoluble. I was fortunate in having arrived at a time when all the Bedouin were away, he told me; while I grinned at him vacantly in my foolish mood. Come the summer—three months ahead—I would find Habarut thronged like Mukalla market-day. The oasis then would be a peace-keeper's nightmare, an uproar of a thousand snarling tribesmen squatting in aggressive postures around pathetic little palms, ready to kill for a handful of dates.

The wild date tree bears a fruit the size of an almond, dry and tart as tamarind. But to the Bedouin it is a prize to travel five hundred miles to watch it mature, to cherish when it ripens, to defend to the death. For eleven months of the year Habarut is deserted. Though it flows with such delectable water it lies in the midst of a vast expanse of bare rock, and the Bedouin graze their goats and their camels where they can find greenery, even if the nearest water is foul as bile. But when the wild dates ripen, like children at blackberry time, the Bedouin come in their hundreds: and these sad little trees, shaggy as brambles, are each one claimed and counter-claimed by men as wild and selfish as starving hawks. And how does one prove or refute title to a shoot, which might have sprouted from the ground since the last year's harvest?

The deceptive peace of the vacant Habarut flowed over my mind for a blessed couple of days. Then I girded my loins for the long journey home to Al Abr: via the vile Sanau, the lonely Thamud, and—this time—the other way round to the south.

During my second sojourn at Sanau I was able to fend off clamorous Mahra and equally importunate, if more gentlemanly, Rashid long enough to poke philosophically around among the gypsum hills. The gypsum had been laid down in parallel layers, and the hills rise in a succession of terraces, flat slabs parted by foot-high steps. And these terraces are carpeted with thousands upon thousands of the imperishable relics of stone-age man: scattered flakes of chipped flint, obsidian axes, arrow-points, knives and awls. The profusion of this vast museum is incredible. It covers acres and acres of sun-scorched waste, in the depths of the most terrible desert on earth. And the well at Sanau is a recent development: it is no ancient monument like Thamud or Zimakh: its original pioneer is still in dispute between Mahra and Kathiri; it is probably no more than a hundred years old. So what imaginable ape-men would have come to dwell at a waterless Sanau and knap their flints? Later I saw other rich deposits, at Habarut, and around Jerboa's castle above Zimakh. This whole country must once have been a neolithic Ruhr.

Hurrying through Thamud as fast as we decently could, we headed west for the long way round to Al Abr. After a long day's skimming over a windy plain, through land so arid that there was scarcely a groove to buck the pick-up, the horizon began to display a new feature. Like a low red sunset thundercloud, the tops of majestic sand-dunes peeped over the rim of the vast and level landscape. Nearer and higher they loomed as we sped, running before the wind; and by evening we were among them.

They can only be described as mountains of sand: mountain ranges. They tower four, five, six hundred feet into the sky, straight up from the dead flat gravel, in parallel chains that march away for a thousand miles across the continent. The windward side of the hills is whipped and rippled into a wild mounting sea of waves; the lee slope is a tumbling precipice; and from the peaks, gently rounded like a woman's bosom, plumes of wind-blown dust fly like great filmy flags against the sky. Here and there a grotesque skeletal tree gesticulates halfway up a heaving shoulder, a petrified memento of some climatic aberration. The immensity of these colossal heaps, and the enormous silence of an utterly dead world, clothes the place in an awesome splendour. Feeling like ants among the Pyramids, the four of us made our toy camp for the night before impertinently plunging into the huge sands at dawn.

We had eighty miles of these desiccated Alps to traverse. When the stars began to fade we lowered our tyre pressures and turned our bonnets towards the first pass: a saddle between two mountains. Dunes such as these can only be crossed in the very early morning, or at night; as soon as the sun is up and the winds begin to lash they take on the consistency of pepper. To make any progress at all, the tyres must be half-flat, so that they waddle over the shifting stuff on the principle of a camel's foot. And the only way even then to get up and over the ridges is to assault bull-headed, full-tilt, engine screaming in low gear.

So we let in the clutch and charged. Twisting and writhing between the billowing waves we wrenched our way to the crest of the pass, the pick-up leaping and lurching like a storm-tossed boat, its load of now empty drums clashing and echoing from the sand-cliffs around us. Then came the long slide down the steep lee slope, where the sand collapsed like an avalanche to bear us cascading to the bottom.

The route through the sands linked a series of such passes, separating broad thoroughfares of gravelly flats between the dune ranges, as level as an airfield runway, two or three miles wide. We seemed to be continually crossing from one valley to another, but the run down the corridors between was exhilarating, and we raced each other to the next sand ridge ten miles ahead. Now and then we saw scattered white spots on the flanks of the sand-hills—gazelle! Then the hunt was up. Faraj and Saleh were old hands. Working like dogs they manoeuvred until a galloping buck was trapped between the two vehicles; then we coursed along, veering and backing to keep abreast of the gazelle's lightning jinks and dodges, until it slowed and one or the other could shoot.

Skidding to a stop, the Arabs raced to the crumpled animal, whipped out their knives, and in a minute they had its throat cut and its skin off and the meat tied triumphantly in chunks like trophies to the tailboard. I was squeamish, this first time, but one who has lived on tinned fish for two weeks is not squeamish for long, and the gazelle-hunt became a regular sport on our travels. I even got used to Saleh's exotic habit of chewing the stomach raw, straight out of the still-warm carcass, merely scraping a sort of spinach-puree away with the blade of his knife and stuffing his mouth with fresh tripe.

I was beginning to wonder why everybody, including the unwieldy Legion convoys chose this longer, and more hazardous, route in preference to the other, which I had traversed—what now seemed a long time ago. But as we finally emerged from the last ripples of the dunes, where the ocean of sand laps against the corner of the plateau, I could see why. Ahead of us stretched a hundred and twenty miles of billiard table, firm and flat as slate, and we flew down to Al Abr like birds on the wing, the horizon to the west melting into purple evening haze while the level grey cliffs of the table-land marked our way on the left.

We came to Al Abr after dark, seventeen days and twelve hundred miles after I had fled for refuge into the far wilderness. I now felt like weeping with relief: I was coming home, from the obscure menaces of Thamud, Sanau, and Habarut. And there to welcome me, sitting smirking on my floor, were a lizard-eyed man whose teeth glinted through his beard, and a stalwart youth with moustaches like a Tartar chief.

" Greetings," said Sarur and Bin Huweil. " The wells have all dried up."

SIX

Holes in the Ground

THE Al Abr wells are a row of pits about fifteen feet deep dug in the bed of a sand-river. They tap a stratum of permanently damp limestone. If water is taken out faster than it can ooze in, they dry up. That is what had happened.

The whole of the western Hadhramaut had been drought-struck for months. The Kurab were all gathered at Al Abr because their own water-holes to the south had failed. Groups of pilgrims on their way to Mecca accumulated daily at the customs house; for it was the season of the Hajj. Grumbling clusters of great black camels had wandered in from the Yemen, and strings of thirsty beasts from Saudi Arabia, for there also the thin desert rains had failed. And Al Abr had yielded under the strain.

Years ago, before the soldiers came, the answer would have been obvious. Sarur's Saar would simply expel everybody else; they would tell Kurab, Yemeni, and Saudi, and pilgrims too, to seek water where they could elsewhere, because there was scarcely enough for themselves; they would mount guard on the rock overlooking the wells, and shoo outsiders away. There might be a battle, but God would dispose.

But Al Abr by now was an international crossroads, and it fell upon me to cope with the crisis.

There were four things to do. I must find some other water supply for the garrison, and myself, lest the presence of authority cause murmurs. I must ration the Al Abr water to human throats, and I must find somewhere else for our own flocks of bleating goats and clamouring camels to drink. And I must try to squeeze more moisture from the earth at Al Abr.

The garrison was easy: they had trucks. Eighty miles or so away, on the fringe of the Hadhramaut farm land, there are scattered settlements with diesel pumps, and a few hours' bargaining bought us water by the drum. The rationing was harder, and not maintained without strife. We posted soldiers on the few wells which still secreted moisture and refused all but those who were drawing water for their own personal use. Thirty miles from Al Abr, I learnt, in a ravine in the plateau lay a small but inaccessible permanent spring. I despatched Desert Guards and volunteers to dig out this hole, to make a pathway up to it, and thus open it up to the goats and the camels of Kurab and Saar. The Yemenis and Saudis were told, with regret, that they must take their camels home. And finally Bin Zaid and a gang of his friends got to work with mattocks and trowels in the dry pits, chipping deeper into the spongy limestone to tap its lower levels.

The crisis lasted about six weeks. Then a heavy shower of rain in the north drew off the flocks and herds to seek the fresh grass, Hajj day came and the pilgrim traffic ceased, and the wells of Al Abr recovered when the mob had gone.

In the course of a tour of the Saar castles on the plateau I found myself one morning squatting on the floor of my tent, which I now used in preference to places like Chateau Jerboa, or the Legion forts where I could not sally out for sanitary purposes without precipitating a military parade. Planted around me in a musty-smelling circle was a hedge of straggly beards and ragged robes, with a row of eyes glinting hungrily through the hairy boscage. For I had brought money for the Saar; and the Saar have a keen appetite for cash. Here was Bin Jerboa, sucking slavering at his tobacco-cud; Bogshan sat enfolded in his mummy-shrouds, wheezing with avarice; Masiud glowed hot and eager. There were half a dozen more of them, and I thought happily of the blessed joy of giving, of how childishly pleased these simple folk would be when they heard what I had to tell them.

The money had come from British colonial development funds, for the repair of the Saar water-tanks. These are stone walls, lined with a home-made cement, built like a barrage across the heads of the extensive system of gullies which etches the surface of the plateau. When there is rain, the water runs off the bare rock, the tanks fill; and they last as a rule until the next season's showers, thick, slimy, teeming with life, but wet. In the old days the Saar maintained their reservoirs themselves, when they felt the urge, out of the proceeds of piracy; but now the British Government had come, had forbidden the Saar to purloin the wherewithal, and in return the Saar expected the British taxpayer to subsidise the upkeep of their cisterns.

This part of the plateau was a museum of previous attempts to help the Saar. Here and there lay pathetic heaps of rock-hard cement, which had been delivered at huge expense, dumped until somebody came to do something with it, nobody came, and the next rainstorm put paid to the enterprise. Hundreds of pounds had evaporated in the desert heat, or had sunk without trace down the bottomless gullet of the tribe. In my innocence I thought I would do better than my predecessors, most of whose schemes had foundered on the rocks of Bedouin greed, jealousy, and improvidence. I had sent a messenger up to Bin Jerboa, advising him that I would shortly call to discuss the just and equitable distribution of Government monies amongst his people, and requesting him to place his wisdom at my disposal.

Bin Jerboa, I thought, if not an executive chief (I remembered the Rikaiz affair, still unresolved) was at least the tribe's judge; and as such, who better than he to arbitrate this matter of common interest to his tribesmen?

I was wrong again.

Instead of consulting, as I hoped, the solitary sagacity of the judge, I found myself now at the focus of the concentrated gluttony of the whole tribe.

Making the best of it, I opened the proceedings. I informed

the ring of lolling tongues that I had so much money for the tribe's tanks; that I was a newcomer, and knew little of their individual needs; that I hoped they would help me to apportion the sum I had brought to them.

At once there was uproar—flattering in its enthusiasm but entirely lacking in that good-neighbourliness, that communal give-and-take I had hoped to see. They fought like starved wolves around a dead rabbit. Sharing the morsel would satisfy none—it was only a question of who could gobble the lot. I sat helplessly switching my gaze from one yammering set of teeth to another until Bin Jerboa suddenly silenced the gathering by removing his wad. His Merlin-like voice seemed to stagger under the burden of his years and wisdom.

" Give it all to me," said Bin Jerboa.

I was gratefully admiring his Solomon-like solution—after all, he was obviously the right man to distribute the funds where they would do most good—when something about the demeanour of the other chiefs stopped me in my tracks just before handing the moneybag. It was at once apparent that the Saar as a tribe placed not the same faith in their judge's impartiality, where handfuls of cash were concerned, as they did in matters of more abstract adjudication.

I tried another tack. Bin Jerboa was visibly disappointed.

" Let there then be constituted a committee," I suggested, my voice dropping tiny and alone into an increasingly inflammable atmosphere. " Let us choose, together, a board of five, who shall elect their chairman, and the money shall be placed in their care for allocation according to need."

This was the spark which set the mixture alight.

Completely ignoring me, the meeting exploded into the most furious wrangle I had yet seen. Eyes, teeth, hands and beards were swept up into a whirling storm, from which a shower of saliva spattered over Bedouin, over the tent, over me. Jabbering loudest of all was Bin Jerboa. I slipped outside unnoticed, summoned Hassan, Faraj, and Saleh, and together we struck the tent and lifted it up like a piecrust over the howling cyclone of Saar. Quietly, while they sat raging oblivious in their circle, I folded my tent and silently stole away.

I had a great deal more to learn about the Bedouin before I could safely deploy my funds.

Some months later, when I had aged and grown wise in the ways of the desert, I tried again. I spent some of the cash on a quantity of cement, which I lodged safely in the precincts of a Government fort, and I laid out the rest on a retainer for two or three masons. I then informed the Saar that my cement, and the services of my masons, were freely at the disposal of any of them who cared to partake; all they in turn had to do was provide labourers, accommodation, and food for the mason while he was at work on their particular tank.

A stunned silence greeted this announcement. The chiefs stood aghast at the effrontery of it—that I should expect them to toil with their bare hands at a task which everybody knew was the lot of captive slaves! But I was able to point out that the slaves—or their descendants—were still alive in their midst, now professional odd-job men; Bogshan and Masiud and the others had only to engage them, on what terms they might agree. " But we have no money!" wailed the rag-draped Rajahs. I shrugged my shoulders. By then everybody knew that I knew that the Saar were wealthy men.

Then began the bargaining. They accepted my plan, they said; but I must provide food and a tent, as well as wages, for the mason, and also transport for the cement from the store to the tanks. I agreed to the transport, on condition that the Saar did the loading and unloading. The Saar said all right, but I must stay up on the plateau throughout the operation to see that nobody cheated. I refused this, as the scheme was scheduled to last about six months, but I gave way on the matter of food for the masons.

So, at long last, the Saar reservoirs were repaired. I received no thanks; but my sufficient reward was a lasting abatement of noise.

I later screwed some more money out of Mukalla, and embarked on a wild spree of well-digging. Seeking out that cheery gang of diggers whom I had found at Sanau on my first tour, I engaged them to excavate a long-dead well for the Kurab on the other side of the sand-choked throat of the Hadhramaut. This was a success: at the bottom was water, and Bin Zaid and his brother Nasser, a judge of the Kurab, were delighted. Gleefully I sank a new shaft at Al Abr; which also bore water, but at the expense of the other wells, to the rage of the Saar (for this, too, had been a Bin Zaid project), so we quietly dropped that scheme.

Encouraged by my moderate success however, I extended operations to Thamud. It was enough for me to have disbursed some Government funds at Al Abr for every Arab—not to mention the Mahra—as far as Habarut to accost me on every tour with demands, ranging from querulous whines to truculent threats, that I should do the same for them. But repairing tanks among the Saar castles, or digging out an old shallow well at the mouth of the Hadhramaut, is a vastly different matter from trying to develop the water supply of the Empty Quarter. The oil company, before it abandoned its fruitless search for oil, had found water in deep boreholes here and there, as at Sanau, but at depths ranging down to five hundred feet, and in other places they had drilled to a thousand and found not so much as a sniff. So mostly I warded off the clamour with well-hedged promises, with expeditions into remote corners of the wilderness to inspect sites the Bedouin thought—or hoped—might be worth a try, and by inviting them to make a start there themselves as a gesture of confidence before I broached my small fund. This last suggestion was generally an adequate silencer until my next round.

But at Thamud I thought I might do something. There was a more urgent spur here, too. Thamud was one of three places that still had a functioning pump, a gift from the departing oil company as at Sanau, maintained by myself with colossal difficulty and at outrageous expense. Whenever a pump went wrong, a frequent occurrence, I had to transport mechanics and parts from the Hadhramaut—a journey of four hundred miles in the case of Thamud. When I had just arrived home at Al Abr after a trip to Habarut it was no welcome news to hear that the Thamud pump had broken down again.

I decided, after two or three near-calamities with these sickly

E

pumps, to close two of them down, leaving only Sanau, where I planned to concentrate all my resources, including a huge store of spares and a resident mechanic. But to prevent a general uprising of the tribes I had to provide compensation. So at Thamud I proposed to dig a new well.

Well-digging in a place like Thamud demands a prodigious administrative effort. Skilled men must be recruited, in the Hadhramaut; they must be haggled with; transported to the site, provided with an arsenal of iron tools and a lorry load of ropes, baskets, timbers, pulleys; they need water, food, tents, lamps, pots and a guard. All this is easy enough at Al Abr, but at Thamud it was not easy at all. Having served for some years in the army I had learnt to assume no unnecessary personal responsibility, but to delegate. So I went in search of a manager who would undertake the whole frightful job.

Finding such a mad entrepreneur was my next task. I sought him in vain through the bazaars of the Hadhramaut; one after another the fat contractors listened to my offer, smiled humourlessly and named six-figure sums. But at last I met Musellem, the celebrated bankrupt. Musellem was a plump happy man, clothed in spurious but splendid prosperity and famous throughout the whole Protectorate for the extravagance of his enterprises and the grandeur of his financial crashes. Mukalla was littered with the rusting remains of his omnibus line, inhabited now by families of Arabs and their goats. Musellem had pioneered the road which leads all the way from Al Abr to Mecca, expecting a rich return from pilgrim tolls; but the Saar had promptly claimed all right to tolls at Al Abr, and exercised it ever since, jealously. Only the tangled casuistry of Islamic law had saved Musellem from the bank's foreclosure on all his remaining wealth—which had already been gaily mortgaged to somebody else. Currently Musellem was seeking our sanction to drive a road right across the sandy ocean to the Persian Gulf . . . it was while he was introducing this madcap scheme to me that I seized my chance.

Evading the subject of the road I put my own small proposition to this india-rubber businessman. He was to dig a well at Thamud, running the whole undertaking himself, from personnel to transport (in one of his doubly-mortgaged lorries) down to the last cold chisel. My obligations were to select the site, to provide him with a sentry from the Desert Guards, and to pay him a stipulated sum on completion of his well. If he struck water three feet down, he would have made a packet. And what, he asked, if he found himself still chipping his way through solid limestone three years later? We set a ceiling, or rather a floor. Calculating rapidly in my head, I suggested a limit of sixty feet, at which we could either agree to abandon the project, Musellem receiving his fee nevertheless, or persevere with a renewed contract. Clasping hands we parted, myself to my desert rounds and Musellem to sign on his men. So deeply was he in debt that it was like alms to the poor: thus I consoled my nagging conscience.

Musellem's first well was a triumph, and he made a packet. I had reasoned that any shaft sunk within a few hundred yards of the existing Thamud well, must find the same water, at about the same depth; and so it proved. I felt like Williamson with his diamonds, like Colonel Drake with his oil, as I stood on the beautifully finished coping and regarded my new hole in the desert with its precious liquid cool and blue at the bottom.

Then Tomatum strolled up, stood in silent fellowship beside me, held out his hand for a cigarette. He looked down. He sniffed. " Nice well," he said.

I agreed, modestly enough. He asked: " Do you think this is going to make up for closing the pump?"

Still glowing with pride I said yes, that was the whole idea.

" The Manahil will not think so," said Tomatum. " You are cheating."

" Cheating?" Suddenly the little hole seemed alone and vulnerable; Musellem's well needed friends. " I've given the Manahil their first new well for a thousand years!"

" The Manahil will not think so," said Tomatum again, shaking his head disparagingly. " All you have done is opened up a new hole to the old well. It is all the same water."

I flew to the defence. " They'll get as much water out of this as they did out of the pump."

Tomatum sighed. He personally, he said, was overwhelmed

with admiration at my enterprise and generosity; he had seldom seen a finer example of the well-digger's art. He was merely interpreting to me the feelings of the ignorant Bedouin, which was his job. " The pump shaft is two hundred feet deep," he mused sadly. " That water is comparatively sweet. This water will be as bad as the old well's. The Manahil will not be pleased at all if you now close down their pump."

Gazing miserably down my hole, which now looked like an ignoble attempt to pass off a cheap substitute on to poor but honest Arabs, I asked my adviser what I should do.

" Dig another well," Tomatum told me at once. " Somewhere else, away from Thamud. Then "—tantalisingly—" then we will not have all these annoying Bedouin around the fort."

" Where?" seemed the obvious thing to ask.

" Tomatum shall show you." When the oil company were drilling shot-holes for their seismic survey, he said, about thirty miles to the north, one of the dynamite charges ejaculated a spout of water. Tomatum remembered; he was there at the time—though every other witness had long since left Arabia.

Tomatum's self-confidence was irresistible, and off we went at once, and sure enough after about an hour's drive Tomatum pointed out a row of little pock-marks in the ground marking the line of the survey. But then he began to amble around, muttering, scratching his head. For whichever way we looked there were hundreds of such holes, laid out in a vast grid-iron spread over several square miles of utterly featureless gravel plain. " I know it was somewhere around here. . . ."

I turned to go, but Tomatum was adamant. I must dig another well; and somewhere here there was water; he had seen it. I thought it possible that the Thamud water-table stretched as far as this, and agreed.

The result was one more ruination for Musellem.

After dreary months of hacking grim-faced through harder and ever harder layers of brick-dry rock, in despair Musellem beseeched me to release him from his disastrous contract. That pit remains his monument. A big crater in the Empty Quarter, eighteen feet across and fifty feet deep, is Musellem's mark, to amaze geologists a thousand years hence. The bare desert around is a treasury of countless broken sledge-hammers, blunted crow-bars, chisels bent into horseshoes (who, I wondered again, had dug Zimakh—and how?); the road across the plateau from his home in the Hadhramaut is strewn with his tyres, ripped to shreds. My heart ached for Musellem. He had gambled once again; this time with the desert; and he had lost.

I was travelling one day from Thamud towards the great sand sea on my way home to Al Abr when my party was accosted by a rifle-wagging scarecrow, solitary, starkly silhouetted on a low gravel ridge. His vehemence, verging on desperation, made me pull up in alarm.

"Assistant Adviser!" he bellowed into my left ear. This was a starved-looking creature, zealous, wild-eyed as a prophet. He wore dirty white sacking with a black woollen rag on his head: so he was of the Saar.

"Yes?" I roared.

"When are you going to do something for *us*, Assistant Adviser?"

I had scarcely thought there was a living soul within a hundred miles. "Us" sounded ominous.

Even more ominous, lean men began popping up one by one all around, and determinedly converging on my two lonely vehicles.

I climbed out and sat helplessly on the ground near an abandoned borehole watching the gathering clan, until there was soon a dense ring of them, eyeing me carnivorously.

The first apparition was their spokesman. They were a sept of the Saar, he said, who dwelt in these parts, a place which they called Hazar. They were a large and powerful tribe, I heard: pacific by nature, they were however well armed, great-thewed, mighty in battle and sorely aggrieved. The others nodded vigorously. Moreover, the speaker mentioned it as if in passing, they lived astride the convoy route to the North which was the Legion's lifeline. Two or three of the delegation licked their lips. These, said the leader, the old men, were of course wise in their grey hairs and would not dream of molesting the Government, which they adored; but alas—their young men were headstrong . . . expert marksmen . . . bold as lions . . . and suffering from a sense of grievance.

The conversation having been opened in this suggestive if circumlocutory fashion, the Saar of Hazar fell silent, waiting for me to take up the dialogue. I said little. I skimmed lightly over the potency of the Government's armed strength, its tendency to strike hard and swift when touched; I dilated for a while on the Government's boundless goodwill for all who respected it. I handed the ball back to the Saar, who by now numbered about thirty, with still more wandering up out of the sands in the terrifying way the Bedouin have of materialising from nowhere when least welcome.

After half an hour of fencing, they came to the point. They had been put by God to live in this awful place; it was their home. Because Hazar was not Al Abr, Thamud or Sanau, they had been completely neglected. Week after week the convoys of rations and stores roared arrogantly through their famine-haunted country, without so much as a wave of a hand. Times were hard. Their only water was what they could rootle out of the dry sand-river beds. They were hungry and fed up. And unless something was done soon they would ambush and sack a convoy; and serve the Government right.

Reeling under this onslaught I pointed out that the oil company had sunk a deep borehole only about two hundred yards from where we were sitting, and that the Government had at vast expense maintained the pump for the Bedouin until the Bedouin had dropped pebbles down the shaft and blocked it up.

" Oh yes," said the Saar. " But that was because the Government sent a man from the Awamer to run the pump. All this land—as far as Sanau—belongs to us."

I abandoned my history lesson and asked them what they thought the Government might do to ease their condition.

At once a couple of dozen eager hands clutched me and carried me bodily to my vehicle. Some twelve of the Saar piled on the Land-Rover, the rest hung on to the pick-up like shipwreck survivors swamping a boat. Off we went, borne in triumph towards the heart of Hazar. We stopped at last against a baked pale grey cliff frowning over a sandy watercourse. "Here," said the Saar, "once upon a time there was a well of water—prodigious in quantity, delectable in taste. The hand of God filled it in, in the days of our great-grandfathers. In our fathers' time a great flood uncovered it—for a day—then buried it again. If you would only shovel away this sand," they said, indicating a dune about the size of the Bank of England, "you would be our brother for evermore."

The fairy-tale quality of this lost well aroused my doubts; the head-scratching wanderings of the old men as they shuffled around trying to recollect just where the phenomenon had occurred, reminded me too vividly of Tomatum and his shot-holes. I managed to extricate myself by telling them that when they had located the spot for sure I would come back and look at it again.

I returned, somewhat shaken, to Al Abr, and forgot about the matter for a few weeks. Then one day a mad-eyed youth burst unannounced into the rest-house and introduced himself as paramount chief of the Saar of Hazar. "But," he went on breathlessly while I blinked, "I have enemies, who would cheat me of my chieftainship." Excusing myself for a moment I checked his name against my files and found him to be indeed the son of a recently deceased chief; so far, so good, though there was something about his eyes. . . .

The words tumbling headlong out of his mouth, he made me an astounding offer. He knew precisely where the well was; his father, the old chief, had shown him, within a foot. He would dig it out—and then his tribe would be grateful, and acknowledge him (and he would get the Government stipend, I added under my breath). If I were to provide money, for which he would strictly account—and, strangely, the boy could read and write—plus a lorry to fetch diggers from the Hadhramaut, he would trouble me no more until the job was done.

It was the answer to a prayer; for I had been dreading the logistics of excavation in that remote and forsaken part of the world. Avoiding his eyes, I accepted his terms; we drew up a contract there and then; I lent him a truck, and off he went, singing.

I heard no more for a month or two. Smugly patting myself on the back for the neat way I had pacified those terrible men, eased their woes, and devolved my responsibility, I waited for news that I had struck water once again.

The news when it came was that I had made another nonsense. On my way to Thamud one morning I was ambushed again on the same spot by the same mob. They were furious; they were quite speechless with wrath, a rare state for a Bedouin. What did I think I was doing, they spluttered, I might as well fling my money on the dunes, where at least some of the starving Hazar Saar would find it.

I could only look at them blankly, shaking my head to avoid the spurts of spittle.

" That boy—" they had found their voice, and screamed at me—" that boy is deranged! He is the lunatic of Hazar!"

I rescued most of the money and consoled myself that I had at least achieved two purposes: the good men of Hazar were themselves now convinced of the futility of their scheme, and I had shown them that they were no longer a neglected people. Mukalla waxed bountiful: doles of grain arrived, recruiting teams visited. The Saar withdrew their threats and became positively affable whenever I passed through their miserable land.

For all these flops of mine, I never enjoyed the distinction of actually destroying a well. One of my predecessors has his name enshrined forever in the mythology of the desert for this unique exploit. When I first heard his story it had already drifted into legend, shrouded in the dreamy haze of romance which graces the great tales of the past.

It seems that once upon a time there was an Assistant Adviser who called a meeting of all the Bedouin to discuss some grave matter. The gathering-place was a deep well to the south of Al Abr.

The Arabs came in their hundreds and their thousands and camped around the well.

The Assistant Adviser drove up in his Land-Rover.

He walked over to look at the well. As it was evening, his face peering over the well-head was buzzed by a cloud of insects.

The great man thought of the sickness malaria could bring among these simple tribesmen. He decided to kill the mosquitoes, which lived a hundred and eighty feet down in the well.

Calling for a big drum of petrol from his pick-up, he emptied it down the hole. The Arabs were alarmed at this— but he held up a hand: " No," he said, " the petrol will not poison your drink, for watch—" and he took an oily rag, set it alight with a match, and dropped it down the shaft.

There was a breathless pause.

Then the well went off like a gun.

Thirty fathoms of air pressure compounded the sudden combustion of forty-four gallons of petrol. Rumbling horribly out of the bowels of the earth, a mushroom cloud of smoke arose and sailed on upwards into the sky; followed by a dense mass of fragmented rock, which had been the lining of the well. The thousand Bedouin watched in awe; but as the echoes died away among the distant cliffs, and the pulverised rock settled rattling around them, they began to look at one another and to ask: " What are we going to drink?"

As the Arab story-tellers put it: " So it is said, but God alone knows if it is true."

SEVEN

Not Within the Purview of the Court

THERE was one man in the Northern Deserts with a bigger nose than Sulayim bin Domaish. Its owner's name, confusingly, was Salowam. The nether tip of this nasal prodigy almost touched the point of Salowam's chin. I never watched him eat, but I could only imagine that the thing was hinged.

Salowam was one of the two permanent residents of Habarut. The other was a gum-champing gaffer whose memory was ancestral but erratic in its reproduction. Salowam was at least clear-minded, and he was articulate; and when the time came for me to grasp the nettle of the Habarut dispute it was to Salowam that I turned for a briefing. Salowam was unfailingly courteous, exhaustively informative; and we had several bouts of profound conversation before I realised the reason for his unusual helpfulness. For Salowam was a principal in the litigation that had been in train for some thirty years.

Bedouin litigation is not normally concerned with facts. Facts, as a rule, are judicially noted. But when facts are unobtainable or non-existent, the Bedouin have recourse to empirical methods of adjudication. These, strangely reminiscent of Anglo-Saxon jurisprudence, are probably common to a great number of ancient and unsophisticated societies throughout history, and may well embalm man's earliest fumbling gropings towards a rule of law.

The first stage of an intractable suit is the ordeal by oath. The litigants are enjoined, by the judge or committee of chiefs to whom they have brought their case, to repair to the tomb of some notable saint—and the Hadhramaut abounds with such tombs, of sparkling whiteness and mammary shape— there to swear upon the hallowed bones that theirs is the right. If the case is important, they are required to produce several oaths—men prepared to stake their fate on the justice of their cause. It may involve as many as fifty a side. If one appellant or the other is unable to persuade enough of his friends to swear for him, he loses.

When the ordeal by oath falls down—when both sides keep pace with an escalating quantity of oaths until the whole thing threatens to become absurd—the Arabs resort to the ordeal by fire. This device was proscribed in the Protectorate by the British Government—thus depriving the Bedouin of their ultimate legal instrument—but it persists in the remoter corners, especially in Mahra country. The ordeal by fire consists simply of a red-hot dagger blade applied to the tongues of the disputants. The theory is that a righteous tongue stays moist while a tongue with a bad conscience goes dry: the latter is burnt, the former not. Generally one side or the other concedes before the ordeal is pursued to its end. More often still, one side loses its nerve and fails to attend the ceremony. The Bedouin value their organ of speech.

The interest of the Habarut palms was enhanced by international complications. The Mahra said they were theirs. The leader of the Mahra at Habarut was called, with typical uncouthness, Bin Hezhaz; and as his tribe was currently the most formidable power in the oasis I had been instructed by Mukalla to assume that Bin Hezhaz was *prima facie* the landlord. But this entailed that the oasis of Habarut was Mahra territory: ergo, that it belonged to the Sultan of Socotra. That suggestion alone was enough to bring Bin Hezhaz to the boil.

" What has the Sultan of Socotra got to do with it?" asked this grizzle-bearded, strangely sophisticated little man.

" He's your Sultan, isn't he?" I asked in my simplicity.

" He is not Sultan of Habarut!" Bin Hezhaz was abrupt.

" But—you are Mahra, and he is the Mahra Sultan. . . .?"

" He is indeed our Sultan—and anyone who dares to defame his name must reckon with us—but let him try to lay a finger on our land—" Bin Hezhaz's thumb drew a line across his throat.

The Rashid thought that the palms belonged to them. In olden times, said their spokesman Khuwaitim—a solitary wandering wiseacre who, like Sulayim, appeared out of the blue wherever and whenever there was litigation to enjoy— the Mahra never dared to intrude so much as a nose into Habarut. The Rashid, said Khuwaitim, were lords of the desert. When the Rashid were away in the sands, then all manner of mean and lowly creatures crept out of their holes and slunk into the vacant oasis—scorpions, beetles, and Mahra. But when the Rashid swept down from the north to harvest their dates—why, said Khuwaitim, snapping his fingers, nobody else could be seen for miles!

" So that makes Habarut part of the dominions of the Kathiri Sultan of Hadhramaut?" I suggested, undiplomatic but eager to learn the scope of the problem.

Khuwaitim peered at me as though I was ill.

" The Kathiri Sultan?" he asked, incredulous.

" But you are Kathiris, are you not, you Rashid? And he is the Sultan. . . ."

Khuwaitim drew himself up very tall, like an outraged stork. " We, the Rashid, are *the* Kathiris," he boomed. " That little man in the Hadhramaut—why, we put him there, and "—he snapped his fingers again—" we can push him out whenever we please."

" Whom then do you acknowledge as your sovereign?"

" God."

" And under God—the Saudi king?" I was trying to be sarcastic.

It backfired.

" Yes, him too, sometimes—when he has been generous."

" And when he has been mean?"

Khuwaitim smiled sweetly upon me and said: " The Queen of England."

So the harvest of a few wild dates had already involved two

sultans, one king and one queen. True enough, some Governor of Aden had long ago laid a ruler across a map in his office and discovered thereby that Habarut lay within the domains of the Sultan of Socotra—but Bin Hezhaz, that Sultan's man, had poured ample ridicule on the idea that lines on maps solve the problems of the desert. Fortunately, both he and I shared the desire to avert bloodshed at the next harvest, now not far ahead.

There were other contenders too, I found. A couple of pathetic remnants of a once-mighty tribe, the Afar (which may have given its name to the Land of Ophir), crept gingerly into the fort when nobody else was there and told me that Habarut was really theirs. One of these Afar was Salowam's atrophied neighbour. At one time, said the two Afar, sad and proud as Russian grand dukes, not only Habarut but all the land from the Hadhramaut valley to Muscat had been their realm. Certainly (they admitted under my questioning) the great days had been a long time ago—about fifteen hundred years, I calculated—but what, they asked, was I, the representative of Justice, claiming to do if not restoring the rights of dispossessed people?

I tried to explain that I was concerned with current realities, not with antiquarian research, but the two Afar fossils clung on grimly, to provide me with the worst headache of the negotiations. For, in point of actual fact, they alone had an incontestable historical right to the place—but to whom did the moth-eaten pair owe allegiance?

" To the Sultan of Socotra," they declared, hands on hearts.

I shuddered, and called in Salowam, the toucan-beaked savant of Habarut.

He settled himself comfortably on the floor, hitched his resplendent robes, applied fire to a lump of stone with a hole bored through it which he used as a pipe, and told me at unconscionable length the whole tale of the Habarut palms.

The story was indissolubly complex. Ransoms, dowries, thefts, pledges, bequests and sales—all contemptuous of tribal and national frontiers—adhere tenaciously to every little shrub. There had been meetings, arbitrations, oaths on tombs, ordeals by fire. In the end, said Salowam, a great flood had swept down the valley and carried most of the palms away.

My eyes widened in hope—then surely, I said, the old claims were swept away with them?

" But of course," said Salowam, puffing his calumet and squeezing the words out between his nose and his chin.

" Then these . . ." I waved my arms frantically towards the rustling fronds below.

" Oh," said Salowam, neatly catching a drop from the end of his beak. " These. Yes. These all came up since I settled here. I alone have tended them. These are all mine."

All Salowam's . . . but who was Salowam? What tribe was he?

" I am from the Bait Ali," said Salowam, hand on heart.

" And who under God do the Bait Ali follow? The Sultan of Socotra? Kathiri? The Saudi king?"

" Not the Bait Ali," Salowam sniffed enormously. " The lord of the Bait Ali is the Sultan of Muscat and Oman."

I fled in desperation to my bath, where I read my files once more. There had been for many tens of years a dispute between Her Majesty's Foreign Office and Her Majesty's Colonial Office about just this small place of Habarut. The Sultan of Muscat and Oman was the darling of the Foreign Office; and he loved his Habarut. The Colonial Office, striving desperately to maintain their pink-coloured Protectorate to its utmost squared-off limits, opposed this Sultan on behalf of the only other Sultan they could find in a position to exert a claim of his own: the shag-haired potentate of Socotra.

It was hard enough restraining tribal quarrels from plunging the Protectorate Sultans into war. Habarut showed all the symptoms of an international conflict, with two British Departments of State taking opposite sides.

The reaction of Bin Hezhaz to the pretences of Socotra had already persuaded me that there was no point in upholding them for the sake simply of following the local party line. I resolved to issue a diktat, an *ex cathedra* judgement, in time for the next harvest; and I had the legionaries in their fort to enforce my ruling.

I sat hatching for some time, and in due course my solution chipped its way cheeping out of its shell.

I summoned Salowam, the Afar, Khuwaitim, Bin Hezhaz; and ranged behind me stood the three officers of the garrison.

" The ownership of Habarut," I pronounced, gulping at my own effrontery, " is not within the purview of this court." I was by now sufficiently practised in Bedouin jurisprudence to be able to produce jargon of this kind.

" Any territorial disputes that may exist between the Sultan of Muscat and Oman, the Sultan of Socotra, the Kathiri Sultan, the King of Saudi Arabia—or Her Majesty of England —will be resolved in God's good time." I thought I was doing well: I warmed to my own eloquence. " But the ripening of the dates will also come in God's good time," I said, pleased with my happy turn of phrase, " and we must adjudicate for the present, not for the indeterminate future. I judge that the gifts of God at present maturing in Habarut belong to Salowam "—my praetorian guard of Legionaries frowned down a rising growl from Bin Hezhaz and the rest—" with the proviso that this judgement shall apply solely to the right to harvest the dates."

I paused, and saw from the flicking eyes of Afar, of Khuwaitim, even of Salowam, that I must make things clearer yet.

" The right to gather the dates," I ploughed on, " conveys no *ipso facto* title to the ground out of which the dates derive their substance; nor even to the trees that bear them. Let no one deem that I am pronouncing the soil of Habarut to be the property of Salowam, or of the Sultan to whom he claims to bear allegiance. Only the dates "— I remembered Portia and Shylock, once again—" if Salowam should cut so much as a frond of the tree he is harvesting, if he take so much as a stone from the valley for his house, then this judgement is null and void."

" But what about Habarut?" burst from the lips of Mahra, Rashid, Afar.

" Habarut must be patient," I told them, " until the great ones—the Sultans, the Governments—have completed their deliberations and allotted this place to its rightful owner. Only the dates, this year and next until a higher judgement shall descend, go to Salowam—who alone has tended them."

So I sloughed off the problem of Habarut, with nobody satisfied but with the immediate threat of a harvest war averted—until such time as Her Majesty's Foreign and Colonial Secretaries should have composed their differences.

The Habarut palms were one of a number of chronic diseases of the desert which I inherited from my predecessors, palliated but did not heal, and passed on in turn to my successors to soothe in their turn. For such cankers are incurable; when they infect tribal and Sultanate boundaries they admit of no solution short of the drastic surgery of a conclusive border demarcation, a remedy from which we all shrank with a shudder.

But these ills were, for that very reason, easier to doctor than, say, an intricate Bogshan-type camel case. For with Bogshan one could, and one must, cure it for good and all, if one was not to have the dreadful old man around one's neck for the rest of the tour. The majestic proceedings which involve sultans and monarchs, even though they relate merely to the gathering of a few dates or the grazing of some shrivelled bushes, can and indeed must be always postponed for reference to some entirely imaginary tribunal which these potentates may be supposed in due course to be convening to resolve their differences. They never will; but at least none of the Bedouin expect their Assistant Adviser to parcel out territory behind the sovereigns' backs.

It was therefore a pillar of my policy, whenever possible to elevate what petty tribal squabbles came my way to the level of an international issue—so far as the Bedouin were concerned, I hasten to add, for I never lost sight of the injunction to keep the desert out of the R.A.'s In-tray.

Wadi Alaib is a narrow winding gully, little more than a ditch, several miles long but only a few yards wide and a few feet deep. It scours its modest way through the limestone table-land a hundred miles south of Thamud. When it reaches the edge of the plateau it takes an abrupt plunge of two hundred feet over the lip, to continue in a more spacious and leisurely fashion across the lower levels towards the Arabian Sea. Below the escarpment lies the untouchable land of the Mahra.

Wadi Alaib nurses in its shallow cleavage a quantity of thorn bushes, delectable to camels and goats. Apart from this green-speckled channel there is nothing for miles but the flat dead gravel and nougat-coloured cliffs of the upland desert.

For as long as they could remember, Manahil from the north and Mahra from the south were accustomed to shepherding their flocks to Wadi Alaib when the thorns were green. In the customary Arabian way, the Manahil thought that the place was theirs, and that the Mahra were their guests, for it lies on top of the plateau where the Manahil are supreme. Equally naturally, the Mahra thought it was theirs, and suffered the Manahil out of hospitality, because the main trunk of the watercourse—as far as the sea—winds through undisputed Mahra country, and they assumed that their title to the valley extended as far as its source.

But this difference of opinion never came to a head until one day about two years before I arrived in the Protectorate, when a quarrel broke out between parties of Mahra and Manahil grazing together in the disputed upper reaches. Bedouin quarrels are highly inflammable, and this one burst readily into flame: shots were exchanged, two Mahra killed, some Manahil hurt. The Manahil flew to the hills, the Mahra leapt with their dead in their arms down the cliff into their own sanctuary, where they vanished.

The Political Officer of the time charged in from the north with a troop of legionaries to clear up the mess. All seemed calm: the Manahil were chastened and tractable, the Mahra nowhere to be seen.

Then the real trouble began.

The Mahra—the section of them who had suffered, known as the Bait Suhail—declared a blood feud. This meant that they claimed the right to slay, with legal impunity, two men of the Manahil no matter whom, whenever the opportunity

F

arose. With that little matter disposed of, they would there-after be at peace with the Manahil.

The Manahil, a big and powerful and somewhat conceited tribe, were reluctant to submit to this facile solution. They asserted that they were in fact owed blood by the Mahra, from many years ago, and the latest payment on account merely reduced the debt by two.

The Manahil demanded a meeting, a reckoning, and a settle-ment in cash, in lieu of corpses. With the slate thus wiped clean, the two tribes could then face the murders and wars to come with a lighter heart. It was a simple exercise in book-keeping. The Manahil chiefs appealed to the British Govern-ment to arrange a palaver.

Meanwhile the Mahra, steadfastly repudiating the authority of the British or of any other mortal Power, sharpened their knives, polished their rifles, and stalked the countryside hungry for stray Manahil.

The Political Officer after many months at last managed to convene a meeting, at Thamud, between the leaders of Bait Suhail and the Manahil. And Sulayim came too. This ubiqui-tous counsellor appointed himself advocate for the Bait Suhail, playing upon their manifest ignorance of the wiles of Christian administrators; and, following his advice, the Mahra adopted a posture of firm truculence. The Assistant Adviser sought to force their hands by imprisoning their chiefs until they should come to their senses (as he interpreted that state of grace).

This was the grossest violation of almost every chapter in the Bedouin code of honour. The Mahra had come freely to Thamud, the headquarters of their adversaries, in good faith and under a tacit safe conduct. Their Sulayim-inspired in-transigence notwithstanding, they felt atrociously wronged, and they took commensurate umbrage. Almost all of the Mahra nation as far as the peaceable Bin Hezhaz at Habarut took their side: even the stipendiary Mahra, the Desert Guards at Sanau, tended whenever the subject was raised to wrinkle their noses at the British Government's concept of fair play. Various forms of pressure were exerted upon Mukalla and in due course, with sundry face-saving reservations, the Bait Suhail chiefs were released to their tribe. Another meeting was called, for 15th June, 1962.

This one was my pidgin.

The details had been arranged in advance, with great political skill, by Jim Ellis. The case was to be heard before two wise old men who were personally remote from the conflict and presumably disinterested in its solution. One of these sages was a dotard in a conspicuous state of decay called Daloum, who was not of the Mahra but who lived among them for some reason and who knew their ways. The other wise man, surprisingly, turned out to be Bogshan. I took him up with me in my Land-Rover from Zimakh.

At Thamud the arrangements were superb. Prodigious quantities of rice and flour and oil had been sent up from Mukalla (a hungry Bedouin tribe *en masse* is a frightening thing). The garrison of the fort had been reinforced. A large tent flapped in its shadow. I myself bore wads of currency notes with which to lubricate the wheels of justice.

The Manahil were there in strength. The two supreme chiefs of that formidable tribe were lodged in the fort itself, at once an honour and a precaution. The *hoi polloi* were encamped around, dotting the plain and the ridges with a dark encirclement of clotted humanity by day and a zodiac of camp-fires by night.

I reached Thamud with my asthmatic arbitrator a couple of days before the sessions were due to open. I dumped him with relief, greeted the senile Daloum with dissimulated dismay and settled down to await the descent of the Bait Suhail.

The Legion, expecting a large and enthusiastic delegation, had sent out a couple of three-ton lorries to meet them, at the top of the Wadi Alaib waterfall.

Two days passed, in the languorous manner of days in the desert of Arabia.

Then on the third day a small cloud of dust appeared on the horizon, betokening the advent of two lorry-loads of seething Mahra. The legionaries on the battlements stood to their arms; the Manahil curdled into silent clumps about their fires; the two chiefs watched, happy enough on the parapet of the fort.

Daloum and Bogshan discussed camels with purposeful casualness outside my tent. I watched with dread as the baleful lorries drew up. They stopped.

Out stepped one man.

I thought I had seen the most nightmarish imaginable human forms at Sanau, but this creature, negro-black, tough and stringy as dried meat, with his grease-caked hair trussed in a leather fillet, with his indigo kilt and his skin-wrapped rifle and his belt a-sparkle with bright brass bullets, was truly horrible. His flesh stretched taut over his skull in a skeletal grin and his eyes clenched into a frown of almost demoniac intensity—as I stared at the apparition, transfixed, I saw that he was greeting me. I smelt rancid oil. When he spoke, it might have been in Chaldean.

He conveyed to me, by what I can only think was telepathy, that his name was Saleh bin Matiaa, and that he was a chief of the Bait Suhail.

Here was one of the real Mahra—that dark and hate-ridden people, dispossessed heirs of Himyar, more isolated from humankind than Papuan head-hunters. I was glad there was only one.

As I looked at Bin Matiaa again I saw that his negro colour was in fact dark blue. He was stained with woad, from forehead to toes. I thought wildly of Caractacus. . . .

I hastily convened the court. Bogshan, Daloum, the fort commander and myself sat gravely cross-legged in the tent. I observed Sulayim hovering kite-like on the horizon but I declined to acknowledge his presence. Then we summoned this savage to attend, to give an account of himself and his tribe.

As he sloped in I saw the rag-swathed Bogshan twitch his tatters fastidiously out of the way.

Saleh bin Matiaa's terse message was interpreted into Arabic by Daloum. The Bait Suhail were not coming. They no longer trusted the Government; they put no value upon its safe conduct. Alone, he told us, being himself aloof from the feud—for some obscure but valid reason in Bedouin law—he felt no fear, and he had come on his own initiative to deliver this news.

We dismissed him, and conferred.

It was patently futile to consider applying physical coercion to the Bait Suhail, for there was no geographical way of getting anywhere near them.

But, suggested Bogshan, we had one sanction in our armoury. The only market the Mahra knew was the Hadhramaut valley.

Under the urging of the now nauseously virtuous Manahil chiefs, and with the concurrence of my two arbitrators, I recalled Saleh bin Matiaa and we issued our judgement. We granted the Bait Suhail three months in which to change their minds. At the expiry of this interlude, if no conciliatory word was forthcoming, they would be forbidden the Hadhramaut. They could buy no supplies in the Hadhramaut markets: they could sell no goats: they must exist as best they may in the God-blasted wilderness which was their home and refuge. If any one of them poked so much as an eyelash above the Wadi Alaib watershed, then as far as the Government was concerned his life was freely forfeit to the Manahil or any other tribe inclined to kill. We enjoined Bin Matiaa to return to his people and apprise them of the Government's resolve. He contracted his brows, and held his peace, waiting for more.

And now I pulled out my trump. The dispute, I told him, concerned nothing more than the settlement of a simple blood-tally between the two tribes. This by itself ought to be comparatively uncomplicated: every Bedouin in the whole Protectorate knows to a thumb how all these accounts stand. The fence they all shy at is allocation of territory—an obstacle which, for a thousand years before the British came, they had never dreamt of tackling. In this case, the disputed ditch lay like an enchanted valley between the antagonists. But that, I impressed upon Saleh, neither I nor any court under me would try. It must await negotiations between the two respective Sultans—whoever they might be. The clouds at once began to lift. The whole appalling business had been reduced to simple arithmetic. Saleh bin Matiaa chose his moment to add a rider. In view of his personal repudiation of the stance of the rest of his tribe, he and his family should be exempt from the ban on the Hadhramaut. His own role as sustainer of negotiations, pleaded Saleh, entitled him to special favour.

I looked at Bogshan, at Daloum. The new zephyr of sweetness had mellowed them. They nodded.

I said, " Yes."

I had a letter drawn up for Saleh, signed with my own hand and rubber-stamped with my official mark, his *laissez-passer* through the Hadhramaut police posts.

The navy-blue barbarian wrenched his mouth into its death's-head grin and proclaimed himself my friend for life.

We made our farewells in a climate of sunny cordiality, and I waved to Saleh as he clambered aboard his three-ton truck for the long journey home. Only one small incident marred this happy scene. Just before his lorry started up, Saleh was accosted by Sulayim bin Domaish, who had wandered over casually to pay his respects to the departing Mahra chief and remained with his arm through the open door and round Saleh's neck and his mouth close to his ear for just a fraction of a moment longer than was natural. It was like a vulture hovering over a flock of lambs in a green field.

Then the wild creature was away, in a diminishing cloud of dust.

Sulayim's poison did its work. We heard no more from the Bait Suhail, and they endured our embargo with fortitude rather than trust us again.

But my embryo friendship with Saleh bin Matiaa was to mature, with far-reaching consequences.

EIGHT

Shameful Behaviour

BEDOUIN shed tears of rage over a dessicated bush; they squabble hysterically around the puddles of mud they call water-holes; they declare war for the sake of a goat. Homicide raises anger too, but of a calmer kind: murder is a civil offence, not a crime but a tort, and differentiated from man-slaughter merely by incurring greater damages. Killings, malicious or accidental alike, can be swiftly and easily wiped off the slate by the sudden death of an adequate number of the offending tribe—it is immaterial whether the original slayer is caught up in this process. Often, the blood debt can be expunged by the transfer of an agreed number of camels or goats: this method is preferred in theory, but often unrealis-able in practice due to disagreements about the relative worth of the departed souls.

But all these are minor irritations compared with the hurri-cane of wrath whipped up by camels. Camels are literally life or death to the Bedouin: more vital by far than trees, wells, women or their own brothers. The dispute between two Sultans over a tract of possibly oil-rich land could safely be adjourned *sine die*. But a fight between two Arabs over a camel demanded my immediate, urgent intervention. A camel quarrel within the tribe—as when Saar steals from Saar—can rip it apart. When the dispute overflows tribal boundaries—as when a man of the Kurab accuses Saar of rustling—the war-trumpets begin to sound. And when the row transcends the international frontiers the whole country can burst into flame.

It was really this, the enormous gravity of offences against the camel, that kept the desert so extraordinarily free of thieves. The whole vast area was an attenuated Piccadilly Circus of men and camels, mingling at will. The herds of a man like Bogshan, who owned several hundred of the beasts, would be scattered, grazing where they chose, over tens of thousands of square miles, finding their own way to Zimakh or Thamud or Sanau whenever they felt in need of a drink— Bedouin when watering camels at a well serve all comers, irrespective of ownership, until the last paunch has been filled. It was not the Legion and its forts that kept Bogshan's camels safe from theft—still less was it the Assistant Adviser. It was the appalling heinousness of the crime. Indeed, more than once I heard Bedouin say that the coming of the Government and its soldiers had increased the crime rate in the desert: for the retaliatory rage of the aggrieved man and his tribe was now restrained, in the interest of the general peace, and there was as yet no other effective control to take its place. I believe this to be true. In the days when a raid was scarcely news, petty pilfering was almost unknown. Under the Pax Britannica raids were outlawed, the natural forces of the Bedouin social system held in check, and the small thief came into his own. The Protecting Power preferred larceny to banditry, for the sake of its own blood-pressure. The Bedouin found the new reversal of values hard to understand.

One summer's evening at Al Abr I was rudely invaded by a gang of enraged Saar, led by Sarur, Bogshan, and Masiud. All were breathing heavily with suppressed emotion. Closely at their heels piled in a troop of Kurab, who ranged themselves on the opposite side of my room. In the vanguard of the Kurab were Bin Zaid my Guard captain, and his brother Nasser, the Kurab's judge. Nasser had a thin grey fringe-bearded face balanced precariously on top of a long undulating neck, like a llama. He was gulping to speak: his Adam's apple bobbed like a bouncing ball: but the Saar wore a dangerous gleam in their eyes, and I turned to Sarur.

" The Kurab," said Sarur, " have shamed us."

It is impossible to convey the meaning of " shame " as a Bedouin appreciates the term. It is anathema; it is the ultimate curse which can be invoked when all argument has failed. Shame is a stain which the afflicted tribe must erase, if it is to hold up its head ever again in the community of the desert. Shame is a worse state than famine, ruin or death. To pronounce " shame " on a man is to blight him as a leper until he has been ritually cleansed. Shame reflects a code of chivalry stricter than anything in the courts of Charlemagne or the Round Table. Shame is excommunication.

So Sarur's invocation of the dreadful charm explained the agitation of Nasser and his Kurab. Even Bin Zaid, that chirpy poultry man, was grave.

The story was this. A man of the Kurab, named Kammam, had been lodging as a guest in the house of a man of the Saar called Salem, among the tents of the Saar at Zimakh. Launching an erotic enterprise with a Saar woman, and repulsed by her menfolk, Kammam succumbed to vengefulness and ham-strung a camel of the woman's family.

This was grossly atrocious. A man might steal a camel— it can be recovered. A man might kill and eat another's camel —it has at least done one son of Adam some service. But to ham-string the animal is to cast oneself beyond the pale of God's children. The Saar were pious and righteous in their rage.

Nasser's yo-yo gullet at last caught my eye, and would not be denied. " We, the Kurab," he squeaked in his distress, " do not dispute the case. Kammam has revolted us as much as he has the Saar. We are ready to pay whatever price Bin Jerboa may set, and so purge our shame."

A more abject speech could scarcely have been uttered by any Judge; and the dignity of its delivery must, I was sure, impress even the bristling Saar.

For a while, indeed, I was lulled into feeling that all was going to be well. There seemed to be no conceivable complication. Nasser and Bin Jerboa would haggle, and assess between them the damages at so many camels, so many sheep. . . .

But something was wrong. There was an angry murmur—
the Saar went into a huddle—the Kurab stalked out with
dignity. I took my cue and retired into my bedroom, where I
downed a precautionary gin. Then the Saar called me back.

Sarur spoke. " Well, Assistant Adviser," he said quietly.
" What are you going to do about these dastardly Kurab?"

Confident, I told him. " I shall drive Nasser up to meet
Bin Jerboa, and they can sort the business out together."

The Saar looked at me in frigid silence.

" So," I went on more warily, " the Kurab will purge their
shame."

A derisive snigger dribbled from the Saar.

" The Kurab's shame!" sneered Sarur, really nasty for the
first time since I had known him. " What about *our* shame?"

I had to pause to let this one settle. The Saar's shame?

" Our shame," went on Sarur, " is what we are here for. Let
Nasser and his Kurab go to Bin Jerboa—that is simple, and a
matter of course. But somebody must purge *us* too."

It took me a long time to penetrate this thickening juris-
prudential forest. It seemed that by harbouring as his guest
a man who had done this base thing, Kammam's host—Salem
of the Saar—had contracted the dreaded contagion himself
. . . and individual shame can adhere like tar to every other
member of the infected man's tribe . . . my mind reeled. The
Saar were commanding me to take action to lift the curse
from them, a curse entirely separate and distinct from that of
Kammam and the Kurab, and a curse which as far as I could
see had been invoked upon them by nobody but themselves.

So the Kurab must do more than simply submit to Bin
Jerboa's judgement on the ham-strung camel?

" Of course," said Sarur, comfortably. The Saar nodded
in smug assent.

It was then that I detected a glint of something deeper than
plain injured honour in the visage of the Saar. Sarur was
flicking his eyes from me to his men, as if weighing my I.Q.
against theirs. Masiud seemed aglow with some hot and angry
feeling, a hound eager for his fox. And there in the corner
huddled Bogshan, and he was actually drooling. The Saar, I

now perceived, were girding themselves for the modern version of a camel-raid—they were going to sue the Kurab from Zimakh to Mukalla, from now until Domesday, for the last ounce of flesh.

I passed a useful day or two in private consultations with the fort commander, with a selection of assorted wiseacres, and with Bin Zaid, trying to wrap my mind around the extraordinary convolutions of the Saar's pleading. Then I stepped into my Land-Rover and drove off to seek Nasser, the Judge of the Kurab.

Nasser was *en famille* on the edge of the sand-plug south of Al Abr. I found him in his tent, a four-foot high homestead of coarse weave black goat's wool propped up here and there by a random array of forked sticks. Little white goats wandered in and bleated and ambled out again. Now and then an onyx-eyed girl of astonishing charm floated in with a bowl of milk or a dish of dates, and silently melted into the rear of the household. Nasser sat, looking like a relaxed ostrich, grizzled eyebrows lifted in mild astonishment at what I was saying.

Over lunch I tried to describe to this eminently wise man the posture adopted by the greedy Saar. Nasser's eyebrows rose higher and higher, his throat undulated like a great pulse, while he fed. Pushing his hand into a thick mass of warm dough in a tin pot he pulled out a lump. Using one finger and thumb he fashioned it skilfully into a sort of spoon. He dipped this soggy scoop into a bowl of pale grey grease which was oozing around a boiled goat, and carried the stuff to his mouth, as one consuming soup. In went spoon and all. He munched. I tried the same trick: my spoon flopped wanly over my fingers, a Salvador Dali sort of spoon. I made a stiffer spoon and dunked it into the leprous broth and bore it reluctantly to my lips.

When the mouthful was safely down and showing no signs of resurrection I resumed my interview. What would Nasser and his Kurab propose, to meet the impending demands of the Saar?

" Nothing," snapped Nasser. " The whole case is absurd. One

of our boys has disgraced himself; we admit it and we offer compensation. What else is there?"

"But Sarur says—" I groped wildly amongst my Arabic to explain—"that the Kurab must also compensate the Saar for Salem's disgrace—the guest and the host—" I faltered.

"Easy," said Nasser. "I know what they are trying to do. Our man Kammam shall sign a statement saying that he absolves unconditionally his host, Salem, from any taint of his own shame, and from any guilt by association. He shall do it now." Nasser bobbed briskly out of his tent and yelled for Kammam. The shame-faced youth came running up from a nearby tent. Before I could finish my next ladle of dough the document had been scribbled (by my driver to Nasser's dictation), Kammam had inked his thumb and signed it, Nasser had made a squiggle and endorsed it, and I had been swept into applying my own mark and so authorising it.

Armed with this confession and absolution I drove back to Zimakh, where I knew I had only to stop and unscrew the radiator cap of my Land-Rover to summon a full convocation of Saar.

"Look what I've got!" I shouted at them in my joy. "Your shame is purged!"

The Saar settled themselves under the great thorn tree; they passed the paper from hand to hand and murmured in satisfied disgust.

"Oh, yes," said Sarur. "Very nice. So Salem is clean again. But what about the rest of us?"

I stared.

Bogshan then opened his phlegm-choked throat and spoke, bubblingly. "Let Kammam and Salem settle their differences. That is nothing to us. You, Assistant Adviser, shall bring the Kurab to settle with us as a tribe—or—" and he nodded at Sarur.

Sarur obediently fumbled in his bullet-belt and drew out a screwed-up letter. It was addressed in the most ornately obsequious terms, to His Excellency the Resident Adviser and British Agent, copy to the Qaiti Sultan of Mukalla. It demanded the expulsion of the Kurab from the homeland of the Saar—which included Al Abr—because of the persistent refusal of the Kurab to co-exist with civilised tribes in a civilised fashion.

" Or else," said Sarur, " we shall be compelled to cleanse our own land ourselves." He blew casually down the muzzle of his rifle. The assembled Saar fingered brass bullets in their belts, and ran thumbs up and down the knives they wore.

Time: two days later. Scene: under the trees at Zimakh. A grey-white circle of seated Saar occupies the largest shade, a ring of conspiratorial mushrooms. From the sinister fairy-ring arises a subdued but audibly indignant murmuration. Rifles point skywards in a circular fence.

I drive up with my pick-up full of ill-tempered Kurab. In my Land-Rover beside me is a stiff-necked Nasser, who clearly thinks it all a contemptible waste of time; Kammam, sulkily aware that he is the cause of the trouble, lolls in the back, with Kammam's clan chief, a violently volatile youth named Asker whose choleric nature is a match for Masiud's. It was a struggle persuading the Kurab to attend, but they are confident that I will put the swindling Saar in their place. I am less sure.

We choose our own shade a hundred yards from the Saar and sit down in a circle, me and my Kurab. Every now and then we peer over our shoulders at the simmering Saar, catch a glittering Saar eye and hastily turn inwards again. The red and white Legion flag seems a very long way away on its fort on the knoll.

After perhaps half an hour there comes a rustling from the mushrooms. They rise, they range themselves into line abreast —I count at least thirty—and slowly they march across towards us, an unwavering thin white line, Sarur and Masiud in the middle, each wearing his own version of a threatening frown. My party stands up; greetings are exchanged with the ponderous courtesy of eighteenth-century European warfare; the gathering settles itself into two horns, with me in the centre where the horns meet.

Everybody sits down again in a heavy silence.

Then Nasser begins to speak, softly and with dignity. A Judge himself, and far senior to Sarur, he expounds the law. The Kurab have offered all that the Bedouin code and custom requires. The Saar case is baseless.

Sarur replies, just as gently; and for a while there is a courtly interchange of legal niceties and arguments. One or two other voices try to join in but are silenced by the interlocutors.

Then suddenly a new note interposes. Asker is leaning forward, stabbing the ground with his finger in heated emphasis, calling the Saar bare-faced thieves!

Nasser restrains him—but Masiud takes up the gauntlet. Asker's clan, roars a blackberry-coloured Masiud, are nothing but a gang of hooligans—Asker shouts back, foam-flecked, Masiud loses his temper, Asker flings his own to the winds and before anyone can stop them the two are on their feet and squaring up, fists on knife-hilts—

Unheard-of behaviour. Two Kurab leap to drag Asker off and two Saar pounce on Masiud. Screams of rage gush from the lips of the duellers—then a Saar says something rude to a Kurab—and the whole crowd fly to their feet in a flash, the Saar hurtle to one side, the Kurab to another, rifles are cocked, aimed—with stark horror on his face Sarur grabs me round the shoulders and hurls me behind a bush.

We sit there, Sarur still clasping me, and I see another Saar chief has Nasser in a similar grip, nearby.

There is a long silence. By the grace of God no headstrong youngster pulls his trigger.

When the calm has lasted about fifteen minutes I get to my feet, still grasped by Sarur, and now Nasser rises and comes over and seizes my other arm. We stride out into no-man's-land, linked together, and sit there. One by one, sheepishly, the others come out from behind their bushes and creep up to us.

The horror of the past moments has swept all truculence away. Rapidly the leaders come to terms. Nasser will fix compensation for the camel with Bin Jerboa. Asker and Masiud shall compose their sudden quarrel before Nasser. The Saar have tacitly dropped their legalistic camel-raid. The meeting breaks up, in an atmosphere of awe.

I drive home to Al Abr and write " closed " against the case.

I was always terrified of murder because of its proclivity to spread like an epidemic. A kills B, so B's brother kills A's father. A considers he had every right to kill B because B's grandfather had killed A's great-uncle; he therefore resolves to avenge the slaying of his father—he shoots B's second cousin twice removed. In no time the whole countryside is up in arms. So it was always urgent to staunch the flow of blood before it swelled into a torrent.

When I heard that a man of the Masadisa, an obscure clan of Saar living in the plateau, had murdered a scion of another family, the first thing I had to do was to arrest as many of the murdered man's relations as I could lay hands on. (The pursuit of the murderer was priority number two.) Luckily they all came in to Al Abr without a protest; they were scared stiff. They huddled shivering around the fort. Then I sent patrols to gather in the Masadisa. It was no surprise to me when the patrols returned to report that there was not so much as a Masadisa goat to be seen. We settled down to wait.

After some weeks of waiting, we got news that the Masadisa chief had surrendered to Bin Jerboa—leading the murderer by the hand. Fearful of an uncontrollable vendetta, they had decided to submit themselves to the more regular justice of the Mukalla Government. So Bin Jerboa sent them down to the Hadhramaut. To escort the pair he summoned three leading chiefs of the Saar and told them to take the Masadisa on their " face ".

Face is the obverse of shame. Sarur and Nasser had taken me on their faces when they wrapped me in their arms at the Zimakh imbroglio: a man's face is " blackened " if anything dreadful happens to his guest, or if his guest misbehaves —Salem's face had been blackened by Kammam the hamstringer. A black face equals shame. Whitening one's face is the same as purging one's shame. And the process can be drastic.

The murderer, his chief, and their three companions set off, in complete confidence that the fearsome sanctions of tribal custom would protect them. But disaster lay in wait. As they made their goat-footed way down the cliff a rifle poked out from behind a rock and discharged. The murderer fell dead.

The dogs of war were loose.

Now each of those three chiefs had a face as black as soot. Each one of them must whiten it with all haste, before he could show it in public. And the only known way they could do that was to kill a member of the tribe of the man who had slain their guest: *one each.*

The original victim's clan now owed three more lives to the other Saar.

The whole thing was ridiculous. I scampered hither and thither in my Land-Rover, from Jerboa castle to Sarur's tent on the edge of the sands, from the Mukalla governor in the Hadhramaut to the family of the original corpse—who were still encamped, now shuddering more violently, at Al Abr.

All agreed. The feud must be cut off at the root. The problem was no longer that of securing retribution for the murder, nor even of apprehending the second killer. What we all had to do, and fast, was to arrest the three chiefs before they could embark on their rampage of face-whitening; and, having impounded them, to find some way of bleaching their cheeks without letting any more blood.

The three chiefs came in to our summons: they were equally eager to solve the awful problem. But the cold body of Bedouin law stood in their path like a rock.

We sat down then, and re-wrote Bedouin law—for perhaps the first time in a thousand years. I was lucky that these men were Saar and not Manahil, or Rashid, or—heaven preserve us—Mahra. They badly wanted to stop the slaughter. Finding such rare unanimity among the usually fractious Saar I could happily tip-toe out from their deliberations and leave them to work out the problem in their own way. The talk turned from blood to goats, from corpses to camels, from *lex talionis* to cash compensation.

The Saar were growing up.

The British Residency, Mukalla. The headquarters of the British Resident Adviser and his staff in the Eastern Aden Protectorate. The building was given by the Qaiti Sultan in 1937, when he signed an advisory treaty with the British

Himyaritic inscriptions on the rockface of the old fort at al-Uqla, south of Al Abr

Monument to a lost race – row of triliths on the way to Thamud

Gateway to the desert – Al Abr Fort. An important watering hole for local tribesmen. Strategically placed on the overland routes to the Hejaz and North Yemen, it accommodated a British Political Officer and a detachment of the Hadhrami Bedouin Legion to keep the peace and mediate in tribal disputes

Wolves of the Desert – warriors of the Saar tribe. Their chief, Sheikh Sarur, is in the centre

Tomatum (standing), 'sharp as a monkey' (see page 50), entertains a couple of desert guards

Road from Zimakh climbing
up to the southern plateau

The Hadhramaut Valley – view from the cliff-top

Shibam – city of skyscrapers – from the air. Its mud-brick buildings cluster in a walled mass, towering sheer to seven or eight storeys. Shibam is one of the three major urban centres in Wadi Hadhramaut and has been included in the UNESCO World Heritage list since the 1980s

Approaching Shibam from the west

Qaiti guard of honour at Al Qatn. This town, formerly the northern seat of the ruling Qaiti dynasty, situated a few miles west of Shibam, was garrisoned by a detachment of the Qaiti Armed Constabulary. Any visiting Arab or expatriate official would be greeted in this way

A stretch of the new cobbled road under construction between the main urban centres of the Wadi Hadhramaut. This project was launched by the author in 1963 and directed by a master mason from Tarim, popularly known as Sa'id Al-Ingleez, who can be seen on the far right

The desert frontier along the southern fringe of the Empty Quarter was garrisoned by a chain of forts guarding waterholes and manned by the Hadhrami Bedouin Legion with the object of preventing tribal raiding and cross-border incursions. Thamud fort was a square functional building dating from the 1950s. An ancient stone-lined well lies outside the fort

Wasteland – the road to Sanau through Mahra country which stretches between the Qaiti State and the border with Dhofar (Oman). A high bleak stony plateau; entirely lifeless

Sanau – notorious for its sulphurous stench and foul tasting water

The Empty Quarter or Rub' al Khali – the vast sand sea extending deep into central Arabia and covering almost a quarter of a million square miles. The first European to cross it was Bertram Thomas in 1931, who was followed by Philby in 1932 and Thesiger in 1946

Mubarak, Chief of the
Kathiri Desert Guards
at Sanau

Bedouin watering
livestock at Minwakh
below the small white fort
manned by the Hadhrami
Bedouin Legion. The
stones lining the well-
head, deeply grooved
by the ropes of past
generations, are indicative
of the well's antiquity

The Residency Office, Sayun. This was a rented building which provided office space for the Assistant Adviser Northern Areas (the author's official designation during his time in Sayun), his deputy and their locally engaged staff. The office was in wireless communication with the Residency in Mukalla

The Kathiri Sultan's Palace, Sayun. The original building dating from the early 16th century was remodelled in the 19th century by Sultan Mansur bin Ghalib, with further modifications to its structure made in 1936. Seven storeys high, the total built area covers some 5,700 square metres

Procession led by the Kathiri Sultan, Hussain bin Ali, and notables about to
enter the Palace on the first day of Eid al-Fitr, the festival celebrating the end
of the Ramadhan fast

Market place, Sayun

Historic Kathiri house, Sayun. This belonged to Sayyid Salih bin Ali al-Hamid, poet and historian and member of the Kathiri State Council, whose meetings were attended by the author

The road to Tarim, a town celebrated for its theological colleges, numerous mosques and the opulent mud-brick mansions belonging to its merchant families. The brilliant red and orange garments worn by the two women in the foreground are indicative of their modest social standing

This minaret is part of the famous al-Mihdhar mosque in Tarim which was founded in the 15th century by an eminent local divine. The mosque was renovated and expanded in the second decade of the 20th century when the minaret (35 metres high) was added. The whole structure is entirely built of mud-brick

Mosque in the old quarter of Sayun. Pictures of this fine example of local mud-brick architecture have appeared in books by several European travellers, notably Van der Meulen and Harold Ingrams

Shrine of the Prophet Hud in Wadi Masila – scene of an annual pilgrimage and fair. Hud is generally thought to be the patriarch Eber of Genesis, and in Muslim theology was the prophet of the giant race of Ád

The author with Colonel Pat Gray, Commandant of the Hadhrami Bedouin Legion

The Qaiti Sultan's seafront palace in Mukalla, whose architecture reflects the dynasty's close connections with Hyderabad. Its spacious compound was a favoured venue for sporting events and military parades

View of the waterfront at Mukalla, capital of the Qaiti Sultanate which had strong maritime links with the Indian subcontinent and East Africa

NINE

"Open up Mahra Country"

In Aden to the hum of air conditioners, in Mukalla to the strains of a violin, and on Socotra to the mooing of primitive cows, history was being forged. Flitting hither and thither dim crew-cut figures, whose accents clashed painfully with the cultured tones of Her Majesty's Government, were sowing seeds of exciting potential.

An American oil company was making a bid for the Protectorate.

Meanwhile deep beneath the surface, more subtle currents stirred. Officialdom was beginning to scratch its head about the inevitable British withdrawal from Southern Arabia, and wondering how to leave the place in a reasonable shape to survive the cruel world outside those safe pink boundaries.

Both these developments were threatened equally by two stubborn obstructions: the Mahra in their desert hermitage, and the Sultan on his island.

The Sultan of Mahra was a Muslim of some sort, but Kipling's " Land of the Cake Parsee " (" by the beaches of Socotra, and the pink Arabian sea ") could well have been the realm of this remarkable monarch.

For decades the authorities had floated happily along on the conceit that Mahra country was part of the British Empire (as witness contemporary maps), and that the Socotra panjandrum was the responsible sovereign of those parts. (As witness the treaties. One of the signatories to an early treaty

G

with His Highness of Socotra was a learned jurist signing himself " Qadhi of Qishn and Collontria ". Qishn is a town on the Mahra mainland: but nobody seems to have asked where Collontria was. It is in fact the local vernacular corruption of " Inglaterra ": Ultima Thule, by courtesy of the sixteenth-century Portuguese. The Mahra still use the word, specifically for Britain, generally for Christendom. Whether the good Qadhi's jest was coincidental or deliberate, none can now say.)

These delusions had never been seriously threatened with reality, until now. On the latest occasion that the Sultan had visited his mainland, in the company of a previous R.A., both functionaries were summarily locked up in a tower by their graceless hosts and released only when an aeroplane arrived to take them away. There had been one or two heroic but ineffectual attempts to shake hands with other people along the Mahra coast. An explorer or two, in disguise, had bribed their way through odd corners of the country. Jim Ellis and his colleagues had built their forts in the desert fringes to the north. Otherwise everybody was thoroughly thankful to be able to leave the place alone.

Until now. Now the Americans were putting their pens to a treaty with the Sultan, which entitled them to prospect for oil throughout his domains. And now, too, the Government was at last facing up to the fact that it could hardly unleash the Mahra naked upon an unsuspecting world as an example of the achievements of colonial rule.

Early in May I was summoned to Mukalla for what were known pompously as " Talks ". Briefly, Arthur Watts told me what he wanted me to do. Open up Mahra country.

Not least of my difficulties, said the R.A., was the fact that the heartland of Mahra had so far proved entirely impenetrable to wheeled traffic.

The sheer escarpment over which the Wadi Alaib takes its spectacular dive stretches on both sides for some hundreds of miles, till in the east it falls into the sea at a mighty cliff and in the west it merges imperceptibly into the huge walls of the Hadhramaut gorge. There are several valleys and ravines, apparently impassable, cutting through the barrier down on to the level plains sloping to the sea—the stronghold of the Mahra. A river called the Jizza, which derives from the Wadi Alaib and other seasonal tributaries, flows erratically through the middle of the country to meet the sea at Ghaidha, the unimaginable capital city of those hair-raising people. And there is one valley which Jim Ellis and a Locust Control surveyor had once explored in its upper reaches, a cutting which also leads into the Jizza. This is known as Wadi Mahrat.

"Wadi Mahrat," said Arthur Watts, "looks your best bet. Take a trip down it and see if you can find a way through to Ghaidha. Good luck. Oh—" he pressed a bell—"you'd better take some money with you."

Armed with Arthur Watts's imperturbable confidence and a substantial sum of palm-oil I took off for the far north.

It had long been tacitly agreed between Mahra and Government: the watershed marked the boundary of the forbidden land. Wherever our Land-Rovers and lorries from Thamud and Sanau could travel, up to the heads of the north-flowing floodbeds, no Mahra would do more than demand a refill for his water-skin. But it was also understood, quite clearly, that all south from the divide was as sacrosanct as a Sultan's harem.

Wadi Mahrat flows south from the watershed.

There was one fairly sure way of going through, assuming it to be negotiable at all: with a troop of tanks. But I had no tanks. There was one other way which might, I hoped, be tried: the way Ellis and the Locust man had done it before me. If I could persuade enough of the Mahra, Desert Guards and other well-disposed characters, to accompany me—to take me on their face, we could at least see how far we got before somebody shot at us.

The dominant section of Mahra in the Wadi Mahrat is called the Bait Somada, and my Sanau friends belonged to the same clan. So far, so good.

I went to Sanau and cast around for likely allies. Peering out from my window in the fort I saw a grotesque Fagin-nose shuffling purposefully towards the gate. Sulayim? God forbid. Then I saw Ashayer, Captain of Mahra Desert Guards.

At Sanau the guards were drawn equally from Mahra and Rashid, each detachment studiously ignoring the existence of the other. Ashayer was a tiny, shrivelled, incredibly dirty creature with the face of a dehydrated ape. But he enjoyed a reputation unique throughout the whole Northern Deserts, of being uninhibitedly truthful, and a sincere champion of the Government. Ashayer, I thought, was a possibility.

I summoned Ashayer. He squatted like a dust-caked chimpanzee on the floor and listened, in a respectful silence broken only by an occasional croaking grunt, while I spoke. I intended to travel the Mahrat, I said. Ashayer's eyes flickered anxiously. No soldiers, I assured him; I would take only my faithful Desert Guards, to allay the natural fears of the good people of that valley. Would Ashayer, as Captain, allot me some of his men?

Ashayer was blunt as usual. There was no use whatever in going with soldiers—unless I had two or three hundred; and even they could be pinned down in the gorge. Nor was there any point in taking Desert Guards, *qua* guards. They would be treated as rudely as soldiers, Bait Somada or Rashid alike. All I could do was to put myself in the hands of some private Mahra as their guests. Then if there was trouble their whole tribe would be at our backs.

I had hoped for this. I asked Ashayer outright if he would take me on his face: as a civilian, not as a guard.

Without a second's hesitation he said " Yes." " But," he went on, in his bullfrog voice, " myself alone is not enough. My own clan is only twelve men strong. You must take more."

" Who?"

Ashayer reeled off some names, who together represented most of the houses of the Bait Somada. " Bashayer," said Ashayer. I knew Bashayer—a vast smiling man like an amiable Carnera, simple but straight. " Bin Nagi." " Who is Bin Nagi?" " Bin Nagi are," said Ashayer, " the two titular chiefs of all the Bait Somada. Brothers. Bin Nagi must come."

I was totting up on my fingers counting Land-Rover seats.

" Bin Woraiga—he has influence. . . ." I was envisaging having to hire a bus. Then Ashayer's croak went shrill. " Of course, Sulayim bin Domaish."

" I won't have Sulayim within a mile of me!"

" You will not travel a mile of the Mahrat without him, Assistant Adviser."

" But he's a snake!"

" He is a snake, but he is the one man all the Mahra trust when dealing with your Government. For the Mahra regard the Government as a knot of snakes, the more so after their treatment of the Bait Suhail chiefs. If Sulayim is with you, they will say: 'Look, he has Sulayim. Sulayim will watch our interests.' But if Sulayim is not with you, they will say: ' Sulayim would not come with this man. Therefore he does not trust him. So he is not for our good '."

I sent for Sulayim.

I borrowed two more Land-Rovers and a wireless set from Thamud, thanks to Pat Gray, and I set out for my rendezvous with the appointed Mahra companions. I left my pick-up behind, as too cumbersome for the Mahrat gorge, and Hassan my cook stayed with it as too domestic for the enterprise. My black driver Faraj could serve a passable meal. Apart from the drivers and radio operators my only military escort was the commander of the Thamud garrison, who insisted on coming along and made it clear that nobody—especially Pat Gray—was supposed to know. Captain Noah was a wizened old owl wise in the ways of the Mahra, and he resolutely refused to let me commit myself to their hospitality alone. He took French leave for fear of a veto by Mukalla; he had considerable freedom of movement around Thamud (though exploring the Mahrat was not within its ambit), so this was less an act of insubordination than a sort of Nelson eye in reverse.

At dusk we drove into the camp of the Mahra above the heads of Wadi Mahrat. With relief I saw Ashayer, a misshapen but sure-looking bundle of dirt. There too was Bashayer, grinning his huge simple grin. One or two Desert Guards sat around on their haunches, emphatically off duty, chosen for the trip because they represented clans. Shining bright as a beacon in the firelight was Sulayim's nose, and beside him squatted two men, one a callow-looking youth with butter in his hair and an entirely blank face, the other a sharp, skew-eyed dwarf wearing an expression of unnerving craftiness like a mask of Richard III. " Bin Nagi," Captain Noah murmured in my ear.

When we had all settled down in a ring round the fire everybody pretended to be pleasantly surprised at my visit and to know nothing of my mission. They asked me with slightly sinister politeness what had brought me to their camp, here on the very edge of their sanctuary, and they looked at me with eyes expectant and fingers twitching for largesse.

I cleared my throat, swallowed, and struck out into my prepared speech.

A great new age was dawning for the Mahra. For how many centuries had they been oppressed into their own small tract—at a warning nudge from Noah I amended that to their great land—for how many generations had they known no peace, no wealth, no fruits of civilisation? They should consider the Hadhramaut tribes, how they boasted of their schools, their hospitals, their markets, their cities and their orderly lives. Had not Thamud its guardian fort, where even now new wells were being built? (Musellem was still on the job.) And all these blessings flowed like a fountain from one source. . . .

" Government," said a sneer I had not heard before. My speech dried in my mouth.

Peering through the woodsmoke I spotted the speaker. He was grey-bearded and pig-eyed and unfeignedly hostile. His voice was hoarse and his Arabic crude but he had a presence and I could feel the effect his one word had made.

" True," the rasping snarl drawled on, " we would like schools for our sons and doctors for our sick. We want peace, and most of all we want money. But we will not have your Government—or any government."

A threatening stir rippled through my audience. I turned to Noah and whispered, " Who is this menace?"

" Al Nissi," Noah hissed back. " He is powerful. He is a leader of the Bait Somada who live down in the Mahrat. He hates your friends from Sanau, thinks they are sold out to the British. You must reckon with Al Nissi."

I coughed again and raised my voice to reckon with Al Nissi. " You have not yet heard my news, O Nissi." I made a dramatic pause, and received the courtesy of silence. " Your Sultan has signed a deal with an oil company."

I might have said their Sultan had made a pact with Satan. An astonished hubbub exploded momentarily into the night, convulsive consonants and agonised vowels, and then the whole meeting leapt to their feet and scurried like cloaked conspirators to the darkness of a nearby bush, leaving Noah and me to toast our fingers at the fire. After a prolonged chorus of jungle noises, the gathering trooped back, and I saw with dismay that Al Nissi was in the van. They ranged themselves around the glow and waited in silence for the frightful man to speak.

Al Nissi leant forward and poked his finger at me and said : " Where is the signature." It was a denunciation, not a question.

He had caught me off balance. I stuttered : " In Aden—or on Socotra—or—"

" Show us the signature of our Sultan so that we can believe you."

I began to explain that documents like oil concessions were generally kept in safe places in big cities. But Al Nissi swept me aside with scorn.

" We are Bedouin," he spat. " We must see for ourselves. First you want to bring the Government to our land "—he made the word " government " sound like smallpox—" and now you say that our Sultan has signed our land away to an oil company." His voice rose to a cracked squawk. " What right has he to sign our land away?"

At this darkest hour I heard a soft but strangely compelling voice utter words of extreme beauty.

" We Mahra," said the voice, " are the most God-forsaken people on earth. We have nothing but our camels and our rifles. All other men are happier than we are; and what is the reason? They have," it finished in haste before Al Nissi could supply the word with his own pejorative inflection, "— Government."

Looking up in deep gratitude I saw a prune-pursed mouth moving mesmerically beneath a vast headland of a nose.

"We have all seen, or heard of, Kuwait," Sulayim went on. "Of the land of Ibn Saud. Of Bahrein; of Abu Dhabi. The people there have silver dollars in oil drums under the floors of their houses. And why? Because they have oil under their earth. Now we may have oil under our earth. Can *we* dig it out? Can we even dig out water by ourselves, except in the stream-beds? So we must have an oil company."

The Mahra sat stilled. Even Al Nissi was listening, chewing a scrag-end of his beard.

"Now. What oil company will come here without soldiers to guard it, without a government to look after it?"

Al Nissi found his voice. "We want no government!"

But now he found no answering echo. Sulayim held the floor.

"We must have government," Sulayim serenely ignored Al Nissi. "It must come, if we are to have oil. So let us say to this Assistant Adviser, 'Come and visit our land, and then tell your masters of our needs. We have heard what you say about our Sultan and his treaty, and we shall have words with our Sultan ourselves when the time is right. If you are not telling us the truth, we shall find out soon enough, and that will be the end of you as far as we are concerned. But until then we shall trust you '."

Sulayim stopped talking.

Unintelligible mutterings sputtered spasmodically up around the embers; but I saw that Al Nissi was refuted. Noah gripped my wrist.

Next day at dawn we were on our way: only Al Nissi had declined our invitation. And beside me in the front seat of my Land-Rover sat Sulayim, puffing with languid unconcern at his brass-tube cigarette.

A short furious wrangle had sorted out the order of march.

I drove the lead vehicle, with Sulayim and the two Bin Nagi squashed beside me and the other major tribal chiefs—Ashayer, Bin Woraiga and company—heaped in the back. The rest piled into the remaining two trucks, with Noah and Faraj perched where they could find a handhold.

We bounced down into the Mahrat without seeing a soul, and drove for half the day along a widening grey gravel river-bed lined with larger and larger trees. The limestone strata of the plateau fell away on both sides in great tawny-pink terraces. At midday we turned a corner in the valley and pitched over into a narrow gorge cutting through the leprous-white gypsum levels I knew so well at Sanau. Here was water; here were palms. This was Khayas, a magnified version of Habarut, a perennial stream fringed with dense shrubberies of wild date-trees. Fields of lucerne and millet, sloping down from the gypsum cliffs, were being desultorily hoed by lethargic little black men.

" Who are those? " I asked.

" Slaves of Bin Duwais, " said Sulayim and Bin Nagi in chorus.

On the shelf above the river stood a row of mouldering mud forts that might have been made of melting chocolate.

" Who lives there? "

" Bin Duwais, " said the trio.

I decided to wait before asking who Bin Duwais was—or were. We stopped under a spreading palm and climbed out and stretched our limbs in its shade. Sulayim and Bin Nagi draped themselves luxuriously on either side of me, and Ashayer brought me my first taste of sweet water for over a week. We dozed. . . .

Crack. Crack-zing. Pop.

I sat up. I ducked behind the tree, bumping Sulayim and Bin Nagi who had leapt round the other side.

" What's that? " I gasped.

They seemed unsurprised " Bin Duwais, " they said and loading their rifles they promptly dodged weaving away between the trees and into the nearest thicket. A couple of minor Desert Guards galloped up and ranged themselves importantly beside me, grim-faced, while the chiefs stalked towards the bellicose Bin Duwais.

There was a long silence, relieved only by another couple of random-sounding shots and the buzzing of innumerable huge hornets, and then my friends came marching back in triumph across the stream bearing in their midst a bent old man and two scowling youths.

" Bin Duwais," they introduced the newcomers. Then they all sat down amicably in a circle, and at a hint I stepped out from behind my tree to join them.

After a round or two of banal conversation I asked Bin Duwais politely why they had shot at me.

They looked offended. " But we weren't shooting at *you*," they said. " We respect the Government. No. We were shooting at those three Mahra who brought you into our land without our permission." Sulayim and Bin Nagi had been all in a huddle with me when Bin Duwais had pulled their triggers, and I marvelled at their faith in their marksmanship as much as I rejoiced in the inaccuracy of their weapons.

In no time, however, we were all chatting jollily; another Bin Duwais brought us dates and honey to eat; and all was amity.

When I asked Sulayim and Bin Nagi in a whisper what Bin Duwais had meant by " our land ", they shook their heads and tapped their temples and said, " Bin Duwais is a half-wit." It was Captain Noah who took me aside, and told me all about Khayas.

Bin Duwais, said Noah, are Kathiri Arabs; they are fanatically un-Mahra; they own all the forts and all the fields and all the slaves of Khayas, and only the numerical superiority of the Mahra with their uninhibited savagery enables them at times, especially at the date harvest, to dominate the place. If I was determined to proceed down Wadi Mahrat with my Mahra guides, I must expect armed resistance from Bin Duwais and their numerous related clans, scattered remnants of Badr bu Tuwairiq's conquest, who live here and there in small but bristly pockets in all the valleys of the plateau.

This was news; even the honest Ashayer had never hinted

that there were others with a stake in the Mahrat. I suggested gently to my Mahra that we might, for courtesy's sake, and without prejudice to territorial rights, invite Bin Duwais to accompany us on our way through Khayas.

" If you take so much as a goat of Bin Duwais with you," they declared with heat, " we will return to Sanau and you can face the rest of the Mahra downstream as best you may—you and Bin Duwais. Bin Duwais is nothing here, his very life is in pawn to our protection, his claims are ridiculous."

So here was an impasse. But I remembered my box of money, and finding an opportunity to take Bin Duwais on one side I suggested that I should hire two or three of their number, at so much a head, to escort me through their precincts. But, I went on hastily, in order to spare Bin Duwais any unnecessary inconvenience, I would not expect them physically to travel with me. They could do so in spirit, so to speak—at so much a head.

" Five," said Bin Duwais.

" Four."

" In the name of God," said Bin Duwais, and I slipped them the cash and they withdrew. I carried on downstream with Sulayim, Bin Nagi, Noah and the rest, and we made camp just below Khayas, where the going began to be bad.

That night closed in peacefully enough, punctuated only by the strange crackling of the effervescent gypsum rocks. But as the moon rose, one tormented Mahra larynx uttered its uncouth cry, then another, until soon the whole lot of them were in full voice like a tavernful of Chinamen talking Welsh. Noah and Faraj sat anxiously beside me, wondering what was afoot.

After some time Sulayim ambled over to us, with graceful casualness, and the weird chorus subsided. He squatted composedly beside us and filled his brass tube and asked me for a match.

There followed an exchange of trivial chat; and then he asked me, off-hand, " Are you going on down the valley tomorrow, Assistant Adviser?"

I assured him that that was my plan.

He fell silent, smoking placidly, nodding once or twice.

Then: " You know we have taken you on our face, and must come with you? "

Somewhat impatiently I said yes, that was how I understood the arrangement.

Sulayim puffed for another couple of minutes, then with not a flicker of expression he said, " We shall die." He sat quiet for a while, squinting at the glowing end of his cigarette. Then without another word he stood up and shuffled off back to the gaggle around the fire.

Helpless, I turned to Noah, who—wise bird that he was—shook his head sadly and interpreted. " Bin Duwais. You have bought them off; but they have sent word to their relations downstream." I remembered seeing one of them camelling down past us as we made our camp. Noah mentioned three or four other Bins, equally vehement Mahra-haters, equally fanatical about their rights in the Mahrat, who would be lying in wait for my small party.

" Our companions will never admit, even with their last breath, that these Arab tribes have any rights whatever in Wadi Mahrat," Noah went on. " If you insist on going further they must come with us. We shall be stopped. The Mahra will argue; somebody will shoot. With Bin Duwais above us and the others below, you will have to use your money—on their terms. Then more and more Arabs will come, all wanting their share. You might be able to ransom yourself—but our Mahra will die."

" But didn't they know this would happen, before we set out? "

" No. Nobody else has tried to bring the Government here before."

" Then how can we ever pass down the Mahrat? "

Noah shrugged. " With a troop of tanks," he said.

On the initiative of Sulayim I despatched two Desert Guards by camel down the valley, to spread the tidings of the oil concession to the benighted tribes of the Mahra heartland. They had instructions to convoke a grand gathering, an indaba such as had never been seen before in Mahra, of all men of goodwill who might be interested to hear more details of the news and who might be prepared to co-operate in smoothing the way for the company. When Noah heard of this enterprise he clucked his tongue in mingled ridicule and apprehension—for the Mahra are like uranium, a critical mass can explode with a force measurable in kilotons—but I could think of nothing else to do, and after all Sulayim had suggested it. My small success in inducing Ashayer's group to escort me into the Mahrat must have gone to my head.

I withdrew to Thamud, paid off my friends, and took stock. Remembering Al Nissi's demand to see the Sultan's signature, I thought that some sort of firman or passport from the Sultan might save me many hours of arguing on any future journeys, and I radioed the R.A. to see if he could obtain such a document.

There was one strange postscript to this expedition. Bin Nagi, I learnt, had been all set to claim Faraj, my driver, as their own property, until restrained by the wiser heads among the party. Faraj, it seemed, had been brought up from boyhood as a slave of these same Bait Somada. He had been taken from them, while still a lad, in a raid by the Saar (I could imagine Faraj's black ears burning while Sulayim told me his tale); had escaped from the clutches of the Saar, made his way to Mukalla, and enlisted in the Hadhramaut Bedouin Legion. So when he reappeared, in the heart of Bait Somada country, far away from his army and surrounded only by Mahra, the two dull-witted but covetous chiefs had rubbed their hands in secret glee—until the others told them not to be so stupid. I never mentioned Faraj's antecedents to him; but I can imagine how uneasy he had been during that trip.

At Thamud I dug out Tomatum and began to discuss certain matters in a circumspect way. I could not employ him directly in this undertaking, because he was of the Manahil, and the Qaiti Government would make political profit out of his participation; but he knew his Mahra, and he knew their country well from the days of his piratical youth. I was probing subtly into the possibility of another route to the Mahra heartland, a way where the crucial but unavoidable defile through the cliffs lay outside the Mahra boundaries and where the actual incursion into Mahra territory would cross open ground below the watershed.

I think Tomatum must have heard of the substantial honoraria I had paid to my Mahra guides; for though it still seems to me incredible that such a vital highway had never before been revealed, it is even more incredible that none of my predecessors should have asked for it. I suspect that the Manahil had been keeping it up their sleeve, as a golden key to be offered at the right moment for the right price when Government or oil company should be desperate enough to need it. For certainly the walls of the Mahra were proving frustratingly unbreachable. And now Tomatum sold me the key, behind his fellow-tribesmen's backs. Whatever his reasons, the son of Warlike agreed to show me the route.

We both skated delicately around any mention of Mahra. My map showed me roughly where I had to go, well within the territory of the Manahil, in order to find the way to the sea at Ghaidha as open as the Northern Deserts; and thither, putting his finger to his nose and winking, Tomatum agreed to take me.

So I was off again, Noah still clinging to me like a protective parent. This time the party comprised myself, Noah, and Tomatum, our drivers, and my now thoroughly bewildered cook. We set our faces southwards, and ploughed through the Wadi Alaib, and clambered down a long boulder-choked ravine where my pick-up leapt and cavorted like a bucking bronco: to emerge after a day and a night on to a broad bare coke-black steppe. And there on our left, behind us, a solid rampart of rose-coloured cliff stretched levelly away into the haze. We were below the unscalable cliff; and still in Manahil land.

On the dim eastern horizon a promontory protruded to the south.

" Jebel Fart," Tomatum told me. I made a solemn note of the name.

But now my blood was up. Looking at my map I saw that

the water-course down which we had scrambled through the escarpment, and which now spread broad and lazy across the charcoal plain, led eventually into the Hadhramaut valley, some eighty miles below the furthest point downstream that any vehicle had ever penetrated. What if . . . .

So we had the deep delight of driving up to the easternmost frontier police post in the Hadhramaut from the wrong side, like survivors from a flying saucer. The police piled out and pointed guns: "Where have you come from?" they gibbered.

"From Thamud," we told them with glee.

They looked at us; they looked at each other; they looked at the sand, to assure themselves that there were no wheel tracks except our fresh ones which were leading up impossibly from the east. They scratched their heads, and let us through.

The journey had taken three days of incessant toil with repeated moments of near despair, but always Tomatum and Noah contrived to pacify infuriated tribesmen, to ford a chasm, to scoop a path up a barrier of sand or to demolish the fencing of a village in order to get me through. I was a mere passenger, indeed I felt like mere luggage—my only contribution was cash. We found when we reached the main valley that we had used up too much petrol to go back to Thamud, so our efforts were propelled by a powerful charge of desperation. We had to make it; so we did.

After a succession of wide-eyed police posts had waved us past with a muttered "God save us all", we drove through the third evening to Sayun, the sparkling capital city of the Kathiri State, and the seat of Jim Ellis. The glittering electric lights and the rich moist smells of vegetation were a tonic after our mad safari, and when at last we stopped exhausted at Ellis's white colonnaded house and toppled inside—Tomatum, Noah, Hassan and all—I for one felt like Hillary, Gagarin, and Columbus combined. I also stank like a zoo cage and had a face like a hairbrush. My comrades leapt joyously into Jim's indoor swimming pool, and I dived even more ecstatically into Jim's whisky.

I had found the back door of the Mahra.

TEN

The Teddy Boys

" Thou hast fallen into error, O Assistant Adviser." Mubarak, chief of Kathiri Desert Guards at Sanau, always spoke like that; for he was of the Rashid, most lordly, most classical of Arab tribes. " I shall place thy feet upon the right path."

Mubarak was a noble-featured man of immense dignity, unwaveringly devoted to me (my office, not my person) and full to overflowing with magniloquent advice. He now began to explain where I had gone wrong.

Since my surprising appearance in Sayun I had spent many weeks in unproductive dialogue with the leading characters of Thamud, Sanau, and Habarut: Manahil, Awamer, Mahra and Rashid. I had driven deep into the valleys south of the forts, seeking out chiefs amid their goats, camping in caves, eating shrivelled dates and foetid camel cheese.

And these journeys had lately assumed a weird, haunted air. Wherever I travelled on my pilgrimage a spectral figure would soon enough arise from behind a bush, or from the shelter of a heap of boulders, and accost me in a spluttering travesty of the Arabic tongue. I had never seen any of these phantom highwaymen before. They introduced themselves with unearthly names: Bin Fanzukh, Bin Thowairi, Bin Ali bin Amer Shizri . . . all devoted followers of Al Nissi . . . and each one bore the same burden on his lips.

" We do not want you in Mahrat," they said. " Your hire-lings too—they are unwelcome."

Another, more alarming message was that these unattractive folk were preparing their own meeting in the Wadi Mahrat, just below where my proposed palaver had booked its place; and I was left with the clear impression that the rival convocation would be much larger, more single-minded, bristling with arms and implacably in opposition.

One after another the apparitions materialised, uttered their oracle, and faded back into the desert, with a polite bow. One I could have ignored; two I might have shrugged away; but after three weeks of it I felt that the phenomenon deserved thought.

I came to Sanau and summoned Mubarak and told him all I thought he could safely know; and he gently chid me, in his equivalent of Attic Greek.

" Never wilt thou enter the land of the Mahra thus," quoth Mubarak.

He explained. The Mahra themselves were so ravaged by hatred one for another that the mere sight of me travelling into their homeland in the company of A, B and C was quite enough to make D, E and F swear upon the tombs of every saint in Arabia that *ils ne passeront pas*. Fundamentally, the problem was financial: everybody knew that my chosen escorts were being paid, and everybody else wanted some gravy too. When everybody else amounted to some fifty thousand grasping pairs of hands, the thing was obviously impossible. The irony was, said Mubarak, that the wretched Mahra yearned for their new age to dawn; they were to a man really keen on the advent of the oil company, they genuinely envied the other tribes their mild and beneficent governments. But, proud of their unique anarchy, they would rather die than admit it. And each mother's son would shoot rather than let anybody else import the millennium.

Furthermore, of course, there was the Sultan.

" They know of their Sultan," said Mubarak. " They know that if he can, he will keep the money of the oil company in his palace on Socotra, and that they will receive nothing. That

H

is why they know the Government must come. But . . . ."

" But what do we do?"

" Go in with a troop of tanks," said Mubarak.

So I cancelled the indaba, and investigated other lines of approach. I sent a coded telegram over the Legion's wireless to Mukalla proposing that with a few judicious prods we might induce the Mahra—or enough of them to count—to repudiate their Sultan; and then we could arrange for the several clans to sign up with the company individually, so with one blow eliminating their suspicions of the unprincipled potentate and enlisting their native avarice to our cause.

The response from Mukalla was swift and crisp. The British Protectorate treaty was with the Sultan personally, and any change in his status vis-à-vis Whitehall would require at least a proclamation from the Queen in Council if not an Act of Parliament. And the oil concession was signed with the Sultan, personally, and any tinkering with that could lay Her Majesty open to prosecution at The Hague.

After this squelch I withdrew from power politics and concentrated on the issue at a more appropriate level.

Nor were the Sultan and his Mahra the only problem; nor were they the worst.

Mubarak rolled out his orotund counsel.

" The Mahra live here," said he, " but so do we. Many tribes of Arabs—not only the Rashid—dwell in this land." He reminded me, unnecessarily, of Bin Duwais and their friends. " And especially, there are the Khowar." He even sounded frightened of the Khowar himself. " Now we are Arabs," Mubarak went on. " We are not Mahra. What have we to do with that prince of Socotra? Nothing."

It was obviously not the moment to say that the Imperial Power regarded all sons of Adam, within the mainland territory allotted to Socotra, as the subjects of that Sultan.

The frontiers of the Sultanate of Socotra had been drawn in remote dark offices in Aden and Mukalla, and the bizarre monarch himself had small idea of what and whom he was supposed to rule. The quarrel between the Sultan of Muscat and himself over Habarut had been none of his making; and now here was another brou-haha developing in this segment of Arabia that had been allocated for administrative convenience to His Mahra Highness. For so many of the inhabitants of his mandate were no more Mahra than they were Mohawks. To the white-clad officials in Aden the border question had been easy: some intrepid traveller in sheikhly disguise had marked " Mahra " all over his blank chart of these parts, and it was simple then for the proconsuls to equate the explorer's generalisation with the Sultan of Socotra's wilder claims. " Here be Mahra " on the map was authority enough.

And the oil company's treaty automatically gave them the right to prospect (and the Sultan had the right to the income) over a vast tract of desert where the Mahra were perhaps the most conspicuous but by no means the undisputedly dominant sector of the population. Moreover the Mahra themselves had strict and long-established reservations about the degree of sovereignty their Sultan could exercise over them: and the un-Mahra had no reservations at all—the Socotra baron was nothing whatever to do with them, nor had he or his forebears ever made any pretensions to rule them or sign contracts on their behalf.

" Let us go and talk with the Khowar, whose country lies in the very midst of the Mahra. Let us learn their thoughts on this news. We shall find them eager for oil; eager, even, for government, provided it be just. But the Sultan of Socotra? We shall see."

I had to go and talk to those Khowar, and fast.

Mubarak said, " Aye, let us set forth."

So forth we set.

A powerful remnant of the Kathiri conquest, living now in absolute isolation in the innermost core of the Mahra lands, the Khowar over the generations have developed an introspective attitude bordering on mania. As the Mahra fear and detest the Arabs who press around them, so the Khowar slink bare-fanged in the midst of the Mahra. They are possessed of a xenophobia raised to the second power. They have contrived to exist, an enclave of rats in a land of dogs, by adopting and maintaining a posture of concentrated belligerence, and by cohering as tight-knit as a Mafia band. Like Scots and Jews and other self-conscious minorities, they are successful travellers and sedulous gatherers of wealth: they work in the oil-fields of the Gulf, they save their money, they capitalise their savings in splendid clothes and the most modern and expensive weapons. Rifles are their particular pride. Almost to a man they bear the latest models from the factories of Mauser and Fabrique Nationale: high-powered, often automatic; and they have the ammunition to match. They acknowledge no earthly overlord, no Sultan, King nor Sheikh. They are three or four thousand strong.

The Khowar, I thought, as I trundled forth with Mubarak beside me in my Land-Rover, were going to be hell.

We had sent a messenger ahead of us, Mubarak and I, to invite the terrible tribe to meet me and hear my news. Mubarak knew where the Khowar were grazing, and there was little hope of not finding them. As we drove south-east from Sanau far into a network of narrow valleys I had never heard of before, Mubarak checked with occasional passers-by that the Khowar were at home. Flicking their eyes nervously over their shoulders the strangers told us " Yes."

At dusk Mubarak called a halt. We made camp in a small rocky ravine, decorated here and there with sprouting thorn trees, and we contemplated the morrow. I surveyed my retinue: Mubarak, Faraj my cook-driver (faithful Hassan of the long sarong had been left behind again); a wireless truck with two Legion signallers. Altogether we mustered four rifles —for I always made a strict point of never travelling armed in the desert, as an earnest of my inoffensive purpose.

The Khowar, said Mubarak, were assembled in the next ravine, half a mile away over the hill.

We went to bed. I think my escort slept; and I must have dozed off before dawn.

I was woken by rummaging sounds. I raised myself on a shoulder and saw Mubarak and Faraj bundling things into the Land-Rover.

" Wait for me!" I whispered—that half-mile seemed frighteningly short—and I scrambled out from under my blanket.

" Nay," said Mubarak. " Thou shalt not come—not yet. I will visit the Khowar first, to discover their temper." He climbed into my seat and signalled Faraj to drive on, guiding him up the gravelly slope with twists of his hand.

I watched them vanish over the skyline, and gratefully took a cup of tea the signallers had brewed. Bird-like noises—pea putty poop poop—issued from their truck as they strove to make contact with Thamud or Mukalla. Minutes passed—the radio peep-peeped—then my hair rose bristling down the nape of my neck.

A muffled pop-pop-poppity had intruded into the morse. Somebody was shooting at somebody, over the hill.

I chewed my lip, wondering what I would do if I were really Sanders of the Desert. Leap into the wireless truck—charge the Khowar . . . with two rifles, relics of the war? I stopped chewing—the fusillade had ceased.

We waited.

Then over the stony crest the Land-Rover appeared. It trundled down the slope; stopped. Out fell Faraj, and he slipped swiftly under the vehicle and started to probe. He looked whole.

Then Mubarak stepped out unruffled and strode up to me like Elijah bearing prophecies and made a mock military salute and said: " If thou hadst been with us we would now be dead." Having unburdened himself of this appetising intelligence he sat down and began to drink tea. Faraj, emerging dusty but cheerful from under the chassis, said " They missed my sump " and stuffed a chapatti between his black lips.

I felt completely and utterly superfluous.

At last Mubarak finished his breakfast, washed his fingers, and condescended to bring me up to date.

The Khowar had been lying in ambush. He had been certain they would be; so he seized my vehicle while I was still half-asleep, and went ahead to spring the trap. The trap snapped— but as soon as the Khowar sharp-shooters saw that there was no Christian in their sights, only one Kathiri Arab and one black slave, they held their fire. Mubarak ran the gauntlet through to the chieftains, finding them squatting dark-faced beneath a tree, and persuaded them at least to give me a hearing. I was alone, Mubarak told them, I was unarmed— and I was moreover on the face of Mubarak, which meant the face of all the Rashid. So they said they would hear me.

" Let us go forth," said Mubarak.

The approach to the Khowar camp wound along a narrow alley-way between twenty-foot white rock bluffs. It was like a twisting street. And every thirty or so yards I could see clumps of young Arabs, as it were on the roof-tops, now settled on their haunches wearing derisive smiles where a short while ago they had been posted in ambuscade . . . here and there a contemptuous " Welcome to our Assistant Adviser " laughed down at us as we ground our painfully slow way over the boulders between them.

At last we left this unpleasant corridor and emerged into an open arena, a bulge in the ravine, where a great spreading tree a hundred yards ahead sheltered an alarmingly large gathering of magnificently robed men. Mubarak laid a hand on my arm and told me to stop. He climbed out, trailing his rifle, and walked towards the seated crowd, leaving me and my two signallers to be greeted by the Khowar *jeunesse*.

They slithered in a rush down their slopes and swarmed around us smacking their lips, like cruel children baiting a cripple.

The Khowar young are a phenomenon which must surely be unique in this world. They are sophisticated: they have travelled, to the oil fields and beyond. They are wealthy. And they know not the slightest, wispiest shadow of authority or control. They have shrugged off the traditional restraint of their elders, which alone keeps the youth of the other tribes at heel, and they have nothing whatever to replace it. They are nightmare Teddy-boys—armed to the eyebrows.

A handsome boy of about thirteen sporting a brand-new Mauser rifle sauntered with exaggerated arrogance over to the wireless truck and began to poke his finger amongst the equipment. The combination of childish mischief and cold-blooded deadliness was horrible. I saw the two signallers fidgeting with their own rifles, and I was suddenly seized with terror at what the lad might do in his thoughtless game—if he went too far the signallers would have to resist—the gang of toughs would rally round their mate—somebody would pull a trigger . . . " What's this for, soldier?" drawled the youth. " Calling for help, eh?" He twiddled a knob, wanton destructiveness glinting in his eyes. With consummate sang-froid one of the soldiers switched the set on—it emitted an electric hum, and red lights blinked—and he said : " Be careful, you might get a shock." The Teddy-boy jerked away, brandishing his weapon aggressively, but a clatter of laughter from his mates showed who had won that round.

I was flicking my eyes from one sneering face to another, knowing that if one spark should ignite the powder we were dead. These were nature's children; leopard cubs; and I could see no adult to appeal to. " We know what you are," smirked a voice from the back of the pack. " You are an imperialist." He had been to Kuwait, I assumed, and picked up the jargon of Cairo radio. A sprinkling of chuckles followed, this time on us. " You imperialists are on your way out," he giggled. " What are you hoping to do here?"

I bared my teeth in a seedy smile and answered that I had come to talk to their chiefs.

A shout of derision greeted this. " Our chiefs!" This was a great black boy, a slave. " These are our chiefs "—and he pushed the muzzle of his rifle in my face. " Those "—he wagged his head over his shoulder towards the conclave under the tree—" those old men, they don't tell us what to do any more."

I held my tongue. Then a well-dressed, intelligent-looking youth elbowed his way to the front of the ring. The others made way for him; he must have been somebody of blue blood, though he looked like a truant schoolboy. He stood facing me, his rifle butt on the ground between his legs, he cocked his head on one side and said : " I don't like you "— it was the whine of a nasty child. Then he lifted his rifle, and

I had to remind myself that it was no toy, and with slow deliberation he opened the breech and pushed a round up the chamber, closed it, and pointed it at me. My mind rang wildly with parental admonitions about not pointing weapons, even in play . . . .

" What would happen if I shot you?" this monstrous infant asked.

I stared at him. I had never seen anything like him in my life.

" I shall tell you, Assistant Adviser. Nothing would happen. I can do what I like!" he burst out in sudden horrid glee. " If I want to shoot you, I can!"

This was so plainly and so simply true that I had nothing to say. I was wondering desperately how this appalling day would end.

While the boy was searching his fertile mind for some new torment there came a stir on the edge of the circle of baiters— and Mubarak pushed his way through.

Mubarak was untouchable. They could have slaughtered me and my signallers—I thought suddenly of Faraj, but he, a slave, was beneath their consideration and was sitting unhappily in his Land-Rover smoking a cigarette—and there could be no conceivable repercussion beyond a loud squawk from Mukalla. Mubarak, however, had several thousand men of the Rashid to avenge him, and even these emancipated teenagers would hesitate before precipitating a major feud. So Mubarak reached me, and brusquely he told the cub-pack to shut up. Taking me by the hand he led me through their grimacing ranks and alone we walked towards the solemn parliament beneath the tree. I feared for my brave signallers; but the children had had their fun, and now they trailed mopping and mowing behind Mubarak and me.

The Khowar chiefs rose to their feet with icy coldness and let me through, closing ranks behind me so that I was promptly imprisoned within. These were older men, with none of the tinselly veneer of worldly-wisdom which made the youngsters so frightening. These were what I was used to: honest hostile tribesmen, reasonably predictable though hard.

As I walked into the ring, Mubarak still gripping my hand tight, I noticed that the centre of the group remained reclining around the roots of the tree. This was exceptional, a deliberate discourtesy, if no worse. A Bedouin stands to meet his best enemy. But these lolled, and I stood before them like a criminal at the bar.

There were four of them: two nondescript bearded Bedouin, one smart-aleck with a face like a Cockney costermonger and a natty striped shirt; and lying relaxed in the centre, a huge inert rhinoceros, was a great blind man. Mubarak nudged me; and croakingly I spoke.

"Peace upon you," I tried.

There was a long silence. This formula of "peace" is crucial in Bedouin life. If a stranger approaches you and he does not invoke peace, it is best to assume he comes in war, and it may be wise to shoot first. On the same principle, if you meet a stranger and offer him peace and he does not reply—or says "good day" or "nice morning" or some other evasive phrase—it is sensible to presume that he does not wish you peace.

So the pause was critical.

I waited.

Then the blind man opened his mouth and spilt the magic word into the hot noon air. "And the same to you—peace." He made it sound grossly rude, but here it is the letter rather than the spirit that counts.

A gust of released breath rustled round the circle.

I bent down to shake hands with the recumbent chiefs. Four limp hands found mine and wagged, unwelcoming but palpable.

Then I began to work around the ring. I started at one end and I plodded my way round to the other, facing each surly figure, pushing my hand towards him, challenging him to refuse it; I asked after each one's health, loud and clear. Their hands were like floppy rubber gloves, their responses those of a shot-gun bridegroom, but the rebuff I dreaded never came. Once the magic circle was complete I was safe. I was at peace with the Khowar, and they with me, until I left their land; and anyone now molesting me or my party would have his fellows to reckon with.

I sat down like a suppliant before a Roman emperor, Mubarak still faithful at my side, and waited for my cue. Mubarak elbowed me again. It was up to me to speak.

I ran my soot-dry tongue around my mouth, and opened my prepared speech.

It was worse than useless to mention the Socotra Sultan, as I had with the Mahra. To the Khowar, the Mahra were more obnoxious than Jews, and that Sultan as irrelevant as the Pope. So I took another tack.

" The rulers of the Protectorate," I stammered, " have signed up with an oil company." The known or imagined luxuries of Kuwait were enough to make further elaboration unnecessary.

" Which rulers?" asked the stripe-shirted Cockney, quick as a whip.

" All of them—the Qaiti of Mukalla, the Kathiri of Sayun, the Mahra of Socotra."

My tactics were simple. The Khowar owed fealty to nobody —not remotely even to the King of Saudi Arabia or the Sultan of Muscat and Oman. But they lived in the territory known to all as the Protectorate; and everybody knew that there were three Sultans embroiled, with bitter squabblings, in carving up that Protectorate. I thus threw the question of their own position back in their teeth.

They mumbled together in Mahri, like old Highlanders talking secrets in Gaelic, and then one of the grey-beards asked me: " And which of these Sultans has signed for the land of the Khowar?"

This might have been a flattener; but I was ready for it.

" I do not know. All I know is that all three have agreed with the company. This means that the whole Protectorate will be explored—I am not now concerned with which ruler has signed for which piece of it. I hope I can convey to the company your guarantee of co-operation? Otherwise, of course, you may expect them to leave the land of the Khowar out of their survey."

They were quiet for a while. Then the blind man—who was obviously the real power—muttered in the ear of one, then another, of the chiefs. Then he waved a hand, as if scattering crumbs.

Mubarak stood up and pulled me to my feet. " That is all," he whispered. " The Khowar will deliberate."

The circle parted, we walked out and back to the trucks. To my enormous relief the youths had tired of baiting us and now rushed clamorously towards the convocation, to make their horrible presence felt among their elders.

About two hours passed, during which I dared not open up the wireless link or begin a meal or do anything which might jolt the precariously-balanced situation. I sat, listening to the growling groundswell of the Khowar palaver, punctuated now and then by a roar, a screech, or a momentary cat-fight.

Then the hubbub subsided, and I looked up to see a striped shirt approaching me leading a tortoiseshell goat by one ear.

" A small gift," he muttered, almost coyly.

Faraj leapt up and bundled the goat into his truck before anybody could change their minds.

I said I must go back to the council and express my thanks, and, if leave was granted, take myself off.

" No, no," the agitated Cockney shook his head. " Go now —quick." He made shooing motions at me, and jabbered something in Mahri to Mubarak. Then brusquely shaking my hand he scuttled back to his tribe.

As we jolted away through the narrow alley and out to the open desert Mubarak explained it all.

" The old men are grateful. You have brought them good news, you were honest with them, you showed them respect and you have left them to discuss their future among themselves. The young men are the danger. The chiefs are afraid for you, they have no control over them. We are well out of the valley of the Khowar."

Amen, I said to that.

ELEVEN

Christmas Pilgrimage

I LIMPED wearily into my room at Al Abr and the first thing
I saw was Bogshan and Sarur squatting mischievously against
the wall. But I felt like Odysseus, when he came home at last
to Ithaca, and there awaiting him was his old dog Argus . . . .

Since leaving the Khowar I had visited Bin Hezhaz at
Habarut, purchased his good will for a generous sum, heard
his views on oil companies that sign with Sultans without reference to the men of the land, carried away murky threats of
what his tribe would do if they were cheated of their rights
. . . . I had reeled under a volley of delegations from unheard-
of tribes in the deep south, who had picked up strange
rumours and wished to impress upon the Government that
they too had rights. Khuwaitim and Mubarak had expounded
the rights of the Rashid, Tomatum had told me all about the
rights of the Manahil, and a man with the extraordinary name
of Dubb had introduced me to the rights of the Awamer.

Finally Bin Matiaa hailed me one day as I was prowling
around the Wadi Alaib and in the midst of fervent expressions
of friendship and esteem he asked me to renew his *laissez-
passer* to the Hadhramaut—his original had been eaten by a
goat, he said—and he took the opportunity to advise me, for
my own health's sake, not to let anybody overlook the rights
of the Bait Suhail.

Rights, I gradually understood, implied a liberal share in
the oil rentals and royalties. The thought that a miraculous

fountain of gold was about to spring gushing out of their long-dead desert had been greeted with enthusiasm, even by the dour Khowar, but an enthusiasm heavily weighed down with a proviso. If anybody imagined that the tribes would tolerate any of this gold going to Socotra, or to the Mahra (said the Arabs), or to the Arabs (said the Mahra), then let the oil company come well guarded with many soldiers, for it would need them. However, let a just Government but guarantee their rights—and all would be well.

It was good that these simple souls could not see inside a certain small office in Mukalla, where even then a devoted Political Officer was working out provisional estimates for the Mahra State, as though the Socotra Sultan headed a proper government with exchequer and budgets: estimates, moreover, that wrapped up the whole of the tribes' rights into neat parcels, so much for education, so much for health, so much for official salaries, and—so much for the Sultan's privy purse. Even the Sultan was dismayed at this abracadabra, which smacked to him of sharp practice. His budget had always been simple, before the R.A. got down to work on it. All the rights were his, and they should be delivered to him forthwith—in cash.

So the mainland tribes had been perfectly justified in their suspicions. It was unfortunate that they were almost as suspicious of the good faith of the British Government; but Bedouin in general, and Mahra in particular, are obsessed to the point of mental illness by the subject of lucre. As long as nobody has any, they are as happy as Arcadians; but let the filthy stuff begin to stick to one or two fingers, and their baser egos are aroused. And those can be base indeed.

My passport had arrived during these days. Written by hand on a piece of nondescript notepaper with a printed heading: AFFRARIYA GOVERNMENT (the Sultan's family name was Afrar), it said: "To all the tribes of Mahra. Know ye that We have permitted the Mister Allfree to travel in Mahra. Ye are to provide him with every possible assistance, and to ease his path. And accept our sincere greeting. Sultan Issa bin Ali bin Salem bin Saad bin Towari bin Afrar." This missive, engrossed in a baroque Arabic script, was signed with a jagged line and a couple of blobs, which represented His Highness's sole literary accomplishment.

I bore this document confidently on my subsequent visits to the Mahra; but one and all they looked at it, heard it read, passed it from hand to hand, wrinkled their noses and spat.

" Who does he think he is?" they asked.

So sadly I folded my passport and returned to Al Abr, baffled.

And there, like a pair of comfortable old boots warming beside the fire, sat Bogshan and Sarur.

" Good news." They licked their lips. " The Imam of Yemen has been deposed, the republicans are beating the life out of the Bedouin. Now," they gloated, "now is the time to talk to the Dahm."

I had to ask them to let me down more gently: I had heard nothing about any republicans in that epitome of a monarchy, the Yemen. They told me there had just been a revolution; that beastly man the Imam had evaporated; now there were honest clean-living republicans in power, propped up by thousands of Egyptians, decent men who were waging delightful war on the tribes. Especially, said Sarur and Bogshan, the new men were teaching the Dahm their place—

" The Dahm have their hands full." Sarur rubbed his own hands. " They are being bombed. Now is the time to demand a settlement of our claims."

Bogshan drooled.

It was true enough. The very next morning I was woken by an agitated Hassan telling me that the post was overrun by foreign troops. Alarmed, I looked out of my window and saw a convoy of a dozen strange trucks, loaded with boxes of military shape, guarded by a squad of soldiers in unfamiliar uniform. Stalking about importantly was a regal looking man wearing noble robes and a big bush of a beard. I scratched my head, called for the fort commander, and asked him who in heaven's name these were.

The commander seemed as muddled as I was feeling, but

he had been doing some detective work on his own account and he mentioned the name of one of the States of the South Arabian Federation and its Emir. That Emir, it seemed, was anxious to succour the tribes in battle with the republicans, for profound political reasons of his own (not least being a sense of his own vulnerability to democratic pressure). The only way he could deliver his aid, from geographical considerations, was via Al Abr. Al Abr was not only outside this chivalrous Emir's territory: it was well outside the South Arabian Federation.

An urgent telegram to headquarters brought me an equally puzzled acknowledgement, and it was some hours before I was instructed to indulge the Emir's whim—for after all he was supposed to be one of us.

A chorus of agonised bleats burst out from the Mukalla Government customs men, for the privilege of opening or closing their barrier was theirs, not mine; but they too made a virtue out of necessity and merely soothed their outraged vanity by painfully vaccinating each and every one of the Emir's party, including the great man himself, to his chagrin. The convoy ground into gear and lumbered off to the west.

This trespass inaugurated an era of bewildering comings and goings which gave me continual headaches. The Qaiti Government had not recognised the infant republican régime, but it was in no way disposed to compromise its possible future relations with what might well evolve into a powerful neighbour, a neighbour smouldering with revolutionary fervour. Neutrality was their stand, and the apparent active partisanship of their own frontier post must have caused them acute anxiety. Their local representative did his best to make my life a hell, but he realised after a while that there was nothing I could do to stop a traffic which was blessed from above.

The tribes—the Saar and Kurab—were even more furious. The Dahm and the other Yemeni royalist clans were their declared foes, and to see all this material aid rumbling calmly through the midst of their own tribal lands was like roast beef to a Hindu. If the convoys had not been well guarded, one or two would have been plundered: the Saar were hopping with rage. Fortunately the stream dried up for a time, whether from political pressure from our side or mere satiety I never knew. Nothing very much came out of Sarur's peace offensive, either. Bogshan actually made the dangerous journey to the lair of the Dahm, intending to impress upon them that with their preoccupation with the Egyptians they had best compose their feud with the Saar—but he found them so preoccupied in fact that they could scarcely give him a hearing. He contented himself with collecting a casual Dahm camel, and returned to Al Abr.

Soon the refugees began to trickle in, bursting with tales of Egyptian atrocities, machine-gunned flocks, napalm bombs on Bedouin tents. A civilian lorry carrying travellers from Mecca was blown up on a mine. Al Abr was not in the front trenches, but it seemed uncomfortably near them to our tribesmen. They had enjoyed what they called peace for some twelve years, and the outbreak of total war so near their home was an outrage. Slowly, sympathy swung around. The Dahm, after all, were Arabs and Bedouin like themselves, and what was a mere blood feud between friends? The Egyptians were foreign murderers, and all the more heinous for being professed Muslims. Why, even the infidel British never did such things.

The Dahm feud was pushed into the background. If not quite dead, it was placed in suspended animation for the duration of hostilities.

The desert was overawed by the holocaust across the frontier, and a sort of nervous brotherliness settled over our wild men, Saar lying down with Kurab, Asker smiling at Masiud.

My well money was all spent; the Saar on their plateau were repairing their tanks.

I had done all I could with the Mahra, for the time being.

Christmas was coming; and I took some leave.

Christmas in Sayun! The smells were all lime-flower, jasmine, and fresh-watered earth; spiced cooking and camel dung; sun-baked rock and dust. Jim Ellis's house was a symphony in white: blinding brassy whitewash on the sunlit façade, bare plastered walls and a colonnade round the upper floor; cool blue-white in the passages and staircase; soft filtered sunshine in the sitting-room, tempered by wine-red rugs and tinged blue-green like an underwater cavern by the palm trees all around. Rustling fronds, croaking frogs, Arabs greeting the sunset with a wailing song, a back-firing truck, the steady thump-thump of a pump, the startling sneeze of a donkey about to bray—these were the sounds of Sayun. And basking beneath the clear blue bowl of the sky, pinched between two walls of Petra-pink rock, lay thick carpets of sea-green palm groves pierced here and there by the scalding white of turrets, domes and minarets.

After ten months of desert, Sayun was an Eden. And Jim's house was an oasis of Christian food and Christian drink—and a Christian bed. I sank with a sigh into a welter of well-being. I wallowed in comfort like a pig in mud. For Christmas, we had roast turkey and pudding; the bank manager imported —by air—a case of champagne; two or three civil servants from Aden, jaded by their jerry-built suburbia and as eager for the wilds as I was athirst for the gracious life, flew up to join us: and we had ourselves a ball.

It took me three weeks to recover.

During this delirious Yuletide I attended the fair of Prophet Hud.

Hud sleeps in his thirty-foot sarcophagus some eighty miles downstream from Sayun. There, we are told, pursued by his heathen foes Hud tapped on the wall of the Hadhramaut gorge and it opened and let him in and closed, and his enemies galloped past, outwitted. His tomb—a dome-capped white-washed shrine—perches half-way up the precipice, and beside it a monstrous boulder balances, the size of a great house. That is Hud's camel, faithful beast, petrified and preserved for an admiring posterity down through three thousand years.

Below the resting place of Father Hud a town has grown up. Here are mansions, mosques, streets of shops. The houses edge one another up the cliff-side, the alleys nudge elbows

I

down to the water of the stream. It is a city teetering on the edge of civilisation: for the wild woad-painted Mahra a few miles below care little for the Prophet and less for his votaries.

And this town is an empty shell for fifty-one weeks of the year. Nobody goes near it, except the rare caravans travelling down the gorge. Its only inhabitant is a saintly caretaker. Like Lord's in mid-winter, it waits out the time until its season comes around. Prophet Hud's season lasts a week; and afterwards the whole place surrenders again to the bats and the frogs, the scorpions and snakes, and only the watchman keeps his lamp alight.

I had passed this ghostly town on my break-through from Thamud, seeing a mere morgue of dead eyes peering bleakly down at me from their ranks on the cliff.

Now I found myself threading my way through a pilgrimage that would have thrilled Chaucer.

The road to Hud begins as a broad dusty pathway but quickly shrivels to a thin track winding between clumps of salt-bush and colossal fallen rocks. Like sentinels, at intervals of a day's march stand isolated pinnacles crowned with the ruins of the fortresses of Himyar. And as the path shrunk narrower my progress grew more painful. For the citizens of Hadhramaut were on the march, by every imaginable means.

Many pilgrims strode along on foot, like palmers, staff in hand and luggage on head, their festive clothes bleached by the floury dust. Bobbing donkeys tripped down the track with panniers astride their backs and eager men perched on their croups, holding the beast's tail with one hand and guiding it with a stick in the other. Grumbling through the dust-clouds lurched creaking lorries piled to the tops of the side-walls with votaries, feet poking in rows over the side and baskets of chickens clucking miserably at every bounce. Each truck carried its flock of goats, balancing themselves like sailors in a storm on top of the mound of baggage.

Troops of travellers were making the eighty mile journey by bicycle, pedalling steadfastly between the bushes and down and up the gullies. An occasional motor-cyclist belched rudely down the column. Butchers were driving whole herds of sheep along the same thin thread of road, to make their sacrifice to Hud.

And always there are the camels. Proud galleons amongst a fleet of motor-boats and dinghies they sway down the track, with an expression of ineffable scorn on their faces and an entire family on their backs. Father sits in front of the hump, grand as an admiral; mother squats behind him clutching an armful of babies; and slung over the sides in baskets, like boats in davits, ride the children, evenly balanced, goggle-eyed, jabbering at the fun. These splendid argosies sail in majesty through the throng, forcing sheep to scatter, motor-bikes to skid, foot-sloggers to dodge—and drivers to curse.

Through it all, somehow, I made my own way, and I arrived at Hud's town at nightfall. The dead city had burst into exultant life. Lights blazed from the windows; men danced in the thronging streets; coffee-shops blared music; it was fiesta time, and I thought of Hud's thirty-foot long, three-thousand year old bones vibrating to the merriment. I made camp by the stream outside the revelling town and poured myself a drink and toasted the old boy in his hour of fun.

TWELVE

"Shut Up" said the Sultan

I CAME back from several weeks' leave and stepped straight into Jim Ellis's shoes at Sayun. They fitted me like seven-league boots. . . .

The Northern Deserts had been a mere playground, a simple —though spacious—sand-pit where infant Political Officers could gambol with their childlike Bedouin playmates. Or so it was seen in the Residency. Sayun, on the other hand, was real life; Sayun was in earnest. The Assistant Adviser at Sayun was no roving dogsbody as I had been hitherto. He was the accredited representative of the Protecting Power's accredited representative. He deputised for the Resident Adviser on the Sayun Council of State, of which he was ex-officio a member. He was empowered to sign passports, for and on behalf of Her Majesty's Principal Secretary of State for Foreign Affairs. He had an imposing if derelict office building, an assistant or two, several clerks. He administered development projects, and he disposed of considerable sums of money.

In more gracious times this splendid official would have stalked his province in white brass-buttoned high-collared ducks under a Wolseley helmet—if not quite with feathers on top, at least with a spike sticking out of it. It was a measure of the decay of the Colonial Service that nobody even asked me if I possessed such clothes. I took up my residence in the sparkling colonnaded house with nothing but the sweaty old khaki drills of my desert days.

Jim Ellis had some dozen years of Protectorate service behind him when he took over Sayun. I had less than the same number of months. I faced a hard time of reorientation. My period in the desert was of no more value as apprenticeship for this post than two years before the mast would have been. For one thing, I now had to learn to speak twentieth-century Arabic, in place of my distinctly archaic Bedouin speech. For another, I must now assimilate the customs and conventions of an Arab court—in place of the earthy invective and slap-shoulder manners of the desert. And—hardest of all —I faced the prospect of being the Agent of Empire, the Colonial Official, the conspicuous pink-faced deputy of the Great White Queen, in a part of the world where such characters were increasingly regarded at least as tiresome anachronisms, if not—yet—as Aunt Sallies for a hand-grenade shy.

For in the desert, however fractious and exasperating they were, the Bedouin (always excepting the Mahra) nourished a respect and an affection for the British Government that must be rare indeed outside the halls of the Palace of Westminster itself. It was at times touching, at times embarrassing; but it provided the desert Political Officer with a start of a good few yards in his race to make good. If he lost ground, his own flatness of foot was to blame rather than the height of the hurdles.

The Hadhramaut was altogether a different world.

The settled segment of the Hadhramaut gorge comprises some fifty miles of the three hundred mile cleft. Upstream lies the desert, the great plug of sand, Al Abr and the Saar and the Yemen; downstream the valley narrows and fills with water and meanders past the grave of Hud down through a dark and savage chasm to the sea.

The oasis is quite unlike anywhere else in Arabia. It is the bastard offspring of alien civilisations, as untypical of its geographical setting as Albania is of Europe, or New Orleans of the U.S.A. The clothes, the architecture and the cuisine of the Hadhramaut owe more to the East Indies than they do to the land of Mohammed. A Chinaman from Singapore would feel as much at home here as an Arab from the Nejd. A resurrected Himyarite or Sheban, too, would find more familiar landmarks and signposts than would a Sheikh of Oman. The very word " sheikh ", which to ordinary Arabs means an elder or chief, is a derogatory term in the Hadhramaut applied to certain lowly classes of men respected for their piety but despised for their peaceableness. In ordinary Arabic, the title *Sayid* means simply Lord: but in the Hadhramaut it adheres to descendants of the Prophet—men who elsewhere are called *Sherif*. To anyone who knows any other part of the great sub-continent, the Hadhramaut seems a foreign enclave, a kind of huge Chinatown. The yellow skin, the pinched visage, the slanted eyes of the Mongol race are more common among the upper classes than the clear sherry-complexion and the round dark eyes and the Nero-nose of true Arabs. The Hadhramaut is fascinating; but it is not Arabia.

Snuggled beneath the soaring cliffs, three cities and dozens of small towns and hamlets sparkle like crystal in green-velvet beds of palms.

Tarim is a city of holy men, a place of long beards and tall minarets, repository of a fine library of Islamic lore and a citadel of holy bigotry. Tourists who flaunted their foreignness so far as to try to take photographs in Tarim ran the risk of being stoned. Government teachers who tried to instruct the youth of Tarim in the ways of the rest of Arabia and Islam —let alone the ways of the outside world—were denounced. Tarim is over-stuffed with Sayids—in the local sense—a reverend caste of men who wear a special and rather runcible hat, a red fez with a white turban wrapped around its bottom, looking like a tomato-tinted aspic mould garnished with mashed potato.

Shibam is a city of skyscrapers. Built upon an island in the flood-bed, compact and squat, it resembles from a distance a huge iced cake because the white-washed upper storeys of the towering cluster of tenements have run in the rain. Shibam was the favourite view of visiting camera-women. The sewage system of Shibam may have been improved since I last saw the

town; but in those days it was a simple tribute to the force
of gravity. The waste products of the piled layers of humanity
descended under that benign influence through shafts running
the full height of the buildings, and emerged from an orifice
at ground level to ooze slimily down the slopes of the town's
foundations and settle in a treacly sludge into the sand of the
river-bed. The enthralled lady-explorers generally ignored this
aspect of the place. Picturesque Shibam was a slum; the
wealthy merchants and noble Sayids lived outside, in a
hygienic suburb several hundred yards away across the flood-
course.

Sayun is the grandest city of the three, with palaces and
mansions of garish-coloured plaster rising extravagantly from
spacious gardens, and over all the marshmallow mountain of
the Sultan's palace standing as dominant and majestic as a
cathedral over a village.

These three cities were known to us respectively as Rome,
New York, and Paris. I thanked heaven that I was to live in
Paris.

As the swirling broth of tribal wars had finally congealed,
Shibam belonged to the Qaiti Sultan of Mukalla, Tarim and
Sayun to the Kathiri Sultan of Hadhramaut. Sayun is the
Kathiri's capital; it was to him that I was accredited, with
only secondary and rather tedious duties to summon me on
occasion to Shibam.

The Kathiri Sultan is the heir of Badr bu Tuwairiq, that
conquering Khan who overran all south Arabia and whose
memorial is the intricate interlacing of Kathiri weft with other
Arab and Mahra warp throughout the whole Protectorate. The
Sultan of Sayun could, were he so minded, have claimed the
allegiance of Mubarak, Khuwaitim, and all the Rashid of the
Empty Quarter; of Bin Duwais of Khayas; of—so help us—
the Khowar; for all are Kathiris. But bless his heart, he made
no such pretences, and was content to rule his tiny kingdom
beneath the ramparts of the Hadhramaut with no more than
an occasional gesture of sovereignty towards the Awamer.

My first official duty was to introduce myself to the ruler I was supposed to assist to advise. I put on my best khaki and drove off to the Sultan's Summer Palace, a villa in a cool garden. The gigantic sugar iceberg of his ancestors was used only for the most ceremonial occasions, for which the presentation of my small credentials did not qualify.

I suddenly realised, as I wound my way between goats, mud walls and palm-groves, that I had no idea how to address the man. My experience hitherto included two Sultans. I had served the Sultan of Muscat and Oman for a number of years, and as he spoke better English than I the answer was simple: I called him " Sir ". I had also met, in Mukalla, the Qaiti Sultan, but I was only a very lowly guest at a vastly grand dinner and I never had to speak to this one at all. The Qaiti Sultan in my days was a middle-aged pudding, a fifty-year-old with the mental age of twelve. He posed cross-legged like Alice's caterpillar on a mountainous mound of cushions, dressed in a green silk dressing-gown, with a green silk turban perched atop his vacuous face reminding me of one of old Queen Mary's toques. He sat silent except for clearly audible munching and digesting sounds, while the more august guests in his immediate neighbourhood strove to maintain a conversation. The most intelligent remarks I heard that night issued from the cage of a parrot in the background. I was once inquisitive enough to ask how, with a Resident Adviser on the spot with nothing better to do than advise them, the Qaiti people had found themselves saddled with this nincompoop of a Sultan. I was told that the choice was deliberate. The R.A. of the day had pondered, when the previous ruler's death had put the succession in question, and decided that a stupid Sultan would be easier for him to cope with than a sensible one.

But His Highness Sultan Hussein bin Ali al Kathiri was no half-wit; nor, officially at least, did he speak any English. As the gates of his Summer Palace opened and the barefoot sentry presented arms to me, I still had no idea what to call him. " Your Highness " translated into Arabic becomes simply " your height "; " Majesty " is one of the attributes of God; and " Sir " can only be represented by the word " Sahib ",

used by a menial to his master and meaning in actual fact
" friend ". The Bedouin have no such inhibitions. I remember
the Sultan of Muscat being accosted by some of his tribesmen
—loyal unto death—who addressed him direct by his first
name, loudly and with much surplus saliva. The Kathiri's
Bedouin would call him " Hussein " without embellishment.
But to me it would be like calling the R.A. " Arthur "—as
unthinkable as using our own monarch's given name.

Musing on the problem, I slipped off my shoes and padded
in stockinged feet over opulent carpeting towards a small
stocky figure in white gown, snowy silk head-dress, smart
tweed jacket and bare toes. He was sitting in a deep arm-chair
with an elaborate array of elevenses spread before him on a
glass-topped table: tumblers of red tea, dishes of nuts, saucers
of dates. The walls and ceiling of the great salon were a riot
of painted plaster flowers, wreaths and garlands and festoons,
horribly pink and green. Silent black men stood with folded
arms in alcoves. Outside, through tall archways, I could see
the waving green feathers of date palms, hear the babel of the
market place. Inside, the fluorescent lighting was discreetly
concealed, the sofas and chairs expensive. It was a perfect
amalgam of Arabian Nights and Grosvenor House. . . .

The Sultan rose to his full small stature and smiled and
stretched out his hand. Teeth and fingers were aglitter with
gold.

The moment had come. He awaited my salutation, modest,
self-assured.

" Good morning, Sultan," I said.

I was rapidly submerged in a pantomime world. Gilbert and
Sullivan would have had fun with the Kathiri State of Sayun.
There was a Grand Vizier: he sat sipping innumerable glasses
of tea in a small office overlooking the market place, puffing
and slurping and fanning himself. His fussiness, his tea, his
Margaret Rutherford face with its tendency to droop into a
melancholy travesty of Lady Macbeth whenever he was
crossed in political fence, gave every meeting with him a
fresh delight. He was known as Aunty Hussein. There was

an Eminence Grise: a pot-bellied Richelieu named Sumeit, with all the strings of underground power securely held in his podgy hands. Outside the Kathiri kingdom Sumeit might perhaps have been a successful grocer, but within this extraordinary microcosm he was a one-man Establishment. The Minister of Education was a Sayid, a holy man: his name was Sayid Ali. He was lean and intense, distinctly Asiatic, with an expression of such transcendental benevolence that he might without hubris have posed for a portrait of Christ. He had been chess champion of Malaya; he still engaged in correspondence contests with moribund international masters. He was wise, he was sweet. He knew not one word of English except the notations of postal chess.

The total population of the Kathiri State cannot have exceeded eighty thousand souls. But here, notwithstanding the vague protectorate arrangements with London, stood a State as sovereign and proud as imperial Rome. Hemmed into a valley five miles wide, squeezed between the alien towns of the Qaiti Sultan, with the wild sands above and the lawless ravine of the Mahra below; with the cliff-tops roamed by Bedouin whose allegiance was a mouthed homage bought with bags of rice and repudiated if the rice was bad—here in this hole in the earth the Sultan and his strange Vizier flew their green and yellow flag, enacted laws, dispensed justice, issued stamps, and did their best to be friends with their Assistant Adviser.

My first meeting of the State Council thrust me even further into the Land of Oz. I was summoned *de par le Sultan* and found myself cooling my heels in an ante-room while portentous murmurations filtered through a closed door. For this was my initiation: I must be sworn in as a member of His Highness's cabinet.

After a few moments the rhubarb subsided, the door opened, and a white-sleeved arm beckoned me inside. With rubbery knees and a mouth full of sawdust I walked towards the head of a long boardroom table lined with standing white-clad councillors, to where the Sultan sat with his legs crossed under him on a chair, boyish-faced, unassuming, but clearly in charge. He scrambled off his seat as I reached him, he stood up to take my greeting. Then somebody thrust a piece of cardboard into my hand. While the rest of the Council swam hazily around in the corners of my vision I gaped at the thing. Pasted on the board was a sheet of typescript, half in English and half in Arabic. It was the oath.

My neighbour nudged my elbow, the Sultan smiled encouragement. I raised my right hand and began hoarsely to read out the Arabic vow. Somehow I reached the end. I found I had sworn to the Almighty to give my counsel honestly and fearlessly to His Highness, to uphold the integrity of the Kathiri State, to divulge no confidences and to succour no foes. The billboard was whisked out of my hand and everybody sat down.

My place was next to the Sultan. Rummaging in his pocket he pulled out a packet of cigarettes and offered me one. I puffed.

Opposite me was Aunty Hussein, an incarnation of the Sheep in *Through the Looking Glass*, looking lost without his knitting. Sumeit heaved his paunch further down the table, leaning across and whispering conspiratorially to a bony man in an aspic-and-mash hat. Sayid Ali radiated his saintly smile upon the company. And at the foot of the table sat Captain Saleh, in knife-creased service dress and Sam Browne and sword with a blue head-cloth draped to his shoulders.

Captain Saleh commanded the Army : some eighty or ninety eager but ill-equipped soldiers who performed ceremonial duties and sometimes marched off to arrest people when the police were frightened to try. (The police were about forty big black men with green head-cloths who swaggered around the market-place slapping children who tried to steal from stalls.) This was the bulwark of the Kathiri State; and nobody since Alexander has ever led an army with more pride and loving care than Captain Saleh, who now rose to address the Council on the subject of new sandals for his men.

I followed the subsequent proceedings in deep bewilderment. I was expected to interject Advice if I felt the urge, but on this inaugural occasion I was content merely to observe.

Sayid Ali asked the Council to approve extra funds for his overseas scholarships. " No," said the Council.

There was a sudden commotion at the top of the table. A gasp of horror had slipped from the State Secretary. With an expression of agonised despair dangling from his White Queen face he spread his hands in supplication and cried: " But I have already authorised payment!"

" And we countermand your authorisation." Sumeit smacked his lips.

" But I have signed contracts with the students!"

" Then you will have to pay them yourself."

Wailing silently, the anguished Aunty sat down and gazed beseechingly at His Highness, who smiled in thinly-concealed amusement and signalled that the matter was closed.

The meeting disposed with despatch of a number of petty points, and each time the Sultan sat silent, smoking, taking no active part beyond steering his cabinet through its agenda. I was beginning to think he was a figurehead; Sumeit's seemed the loudest voice, the dominant mind, bullying and hectoring his own way through. But shortly this sharp-tongued senator became embroiled in an altercation—Sumeit thumped the table and blared, while two or three others jabbered at him querulously. A sudden sharp crack from the Sultan: " Shut up," he snapped—and there was Sumeit with his mouth clamped tight and his tail between his legs.

" I've heard enough," said the Sultan, an absurdly un-majestic monarch. " What we'll do is this." And he told them; and that was that.

His Highness was no figurehead.

Politics in the Kathiri State were primitive in those days. There was no real opposition to the Sultan except from a few disgruntled members of his own family who wanted to be Sultan themselves. There were rivalries; Tarim wrestled with Sayun over which should get a new school first; Sumeit was at war with Sayid Somebody over a diesel-oil contract—for Sumeit was Big Business. The merchants of Sayun fought tooth and nail for the priceless cigarette monopoly. But when things got too noisy for Aunty to cope with, the Sultan merely told everyone to shut up and do what he told them.

There were no party politics, no social unrest, no class antipathy. The economy of the Kathiri State, and indeed of the whole Hadhramaut, was founded firmly upon an ancient rock. The Arabs did no manual work at all. All the work was done by slaves, or people of slave stock. This black-skinned proletariat composed about sixty per cent of the population. Their labour was in high demand : they commanded inordinate wages; there was ferocious competition to engage their services to build a house, to harvest a crop, to dig a ditch. Amongst the Arab population on the other hand, chronic unemployment and increasing penury now prevailed. I knew of one noble-blooded man whose date crop rotted on his trees because he could find nobody to pick it. His own family, several strong young men, loafed around Sayun seeking hopelessly for clean-fingered situations vacant.

This was a new problem. Before the war the citizens of Hadhramaut were wealthy men, comfortably consuming dividends from the East Indies. The War eroded their fortunes; Sukarno swept up the pieces; and a new generation was growing up with nothing to live on and nothing appropriate to do.

Amongst this distressed *jeunesse* the seeds of socialism and even republicanism were beginning to find fertile soil. The schoolchildren particularly were surfeited on radical politics by teachers who had learnt their own lessons by rote in Cairo and Damascus and Baghdad. The six-to-twelves were a bunch of little horrors who gathered in clusters and jeered at me whenever I drove past their schools at break-time. Thinking (rightly enough) that the Egyptian President was the biggest bogey of the British in Arabia, they shrilled " Long Live Nasser " at me in fervent treble; they piped " Down with the Imperialists "; they waved Egyptian flags in my face; they spat —until either my driver or a local policeman sent them scattering into the alleys. Having met the Khowar I was thankful that these small patriots were armed with nothing more lethal than pebbles. I consoled myself with thinking that Colonel Nasser might have been less than flattered by the fact that his only articulate fans were children, but I reflected gloomily that children have a habit of growing up, and these seemed thoroughly steeped in revolutionary ardour by teachers who had been enlisted and subsidised by the British . . . occasionally I complained about these urchins to the State Secretary, and then a stern edict thundered forth to the offending neighbourhood and all was peaceful for a week or two.

I witnessed only one bout of real political fever. The leading social club of Sayun arranged an open-air meeting at which the speaker was to be a smart young man who had recently returned from studies abroad. The club invited me, in my official capacity; but a warning note sounded in the back of my mind, and I accepted as a private individual. The Sultan and his retinue were already seated when I arrived, on a pile of carpets and cushions against a wall in Sayun's main square. Around him surged the populace, standing in clusters, perched on roof-tops, squatting in herds. If I had come as Assistant Adviser I would have had to join the Sultan. As plain Mr. Allfree, I stopped my Land-Rover on the extreme edge of the mob and sat on top where I could watch the orator adjusting his microphone in front of the royal box.

An eloquent flood of abuse suddenly gushed out into the sleepy afternoon.

For two full hours the preacher thumped his tub and sermonised the captive Sultan, *coram publico*. My embarrassment was acute: the text of the lesson was the iniquity of His Highness's association with Her Majesty. Cunningly cloaking his words in a rich mantle of patriotism and loyalty, so that nothing he said could touch the delicate nerve of sentiment which bound those simple people to their ruler, he bombarded the Advisory Treaty and the British protection with every weapon in the rhetorician's armoury.

How he must have wished I was sitting there with the Sultan. But apart from a small troop of flag-waving tinies who danced around my Land-Rover like spring-born lambs screaming " Down with the Ingliz ", his audience heard him out impassively, with almost insulting considerateness. When the zealot had finished his sermon everybody clapped politely, the

Sultan nodded his head in grave acknowledgement, my driver cried " Bravo " and I was sufficiently emboldened to applaud too—drawing sympathetic grins from my neighbours. The Sayun mob, far from being whipped up to revolutionary fervour and sacking my office, melted unimpressed away into the side-streets.

As a rally, it was a flop. The Kathiri State was not ready for such sophisticated politics. For the next few days the little boys were more obstreperous than usual; and then the whole affair slipped quietly into limbo.

THIRTEEN

Mud Bricks and Dropped Bricks

MY bath was a swimming pool, twelve feet across and four feet deep; my lavatory was an upper room with a hole in the floor. Serving both amenities was Ahmed Yao, a black gnome whose father had been purchased in Tanganyika (the Yao are an East African tribe). Faithful Yao was also gardener. And the three functions were intimately intertwined.

Every morning Yao pulled a soggy wad of palm-fibre from the plug-hole of my bath and let the water gurgle away through complicated channels to refresh his cabbages and lettuce. With nimble fingers he blocked up this channel, undammed that, and my 3,600 gallons of bath water performed the last service. Then he flipped the switch of the electric submersible pump and refilled the pool from the well, ready for my afternoon ablutions: a delectable daily dive and float in the stifling heat of the Hadhramaut summer.

For the rest of the day Yao pottered busily about among the vegetables, tenderly feeding them with armfuls of nutriment. This commodity was provided, in person, by myself. Beneath the lavatory, on the ground floor, was a small chamber with a little door, just wide enough for the pixy-sized gardener, and every other day Yao ducked inside with a shovel and scooped up the ration of fertiliser. The system was cunningly devised; for my cook Hassan who lived below me had his own closet at the mezzanine level which channelled his contribution into the same vault. It was a perfect, if introverted, nitrogen cycle.

Nor was this all. The designer of the house had built a public convenience into the wall of the compound. Passers-by taken short were invited to climb a few steps into a small turret and relieve their distress into a cubby-hole underneath, the entrance of which opened on to my ever-welcoming garden. Yao never passed the spot without a glance inside to see whether there were any offerings from the burghers' bowels.

My office, a mile away, was a large and crumbling mud-built mansion with the stairs and corridors continuously thronged with discontented Arabs demanding alms or sympathy from the Protecting Power. Luckily I had an assistant who was an elderly native with inexhaustible patience and no authority, who spent his days in amicable procrastination with the interminable supplicants, conversing with them at length, listening kindly to their grievances, and being regretfully unqualified to solve their problems. One or two deserving cases filtered through this invaluable sieve; the rest, talked to exhaustion, shuffled away, content to have given their grouses some air.

At the end of the morning, which was the end of my working day, an office boy staggered in like a slapstick waiter with a toppling tower of passports in his arms and I settled down to sign them, thinking longingly of home.

For much of the time I successfully avoided the office. Passports and petitioners drove me away to one or another of the projects with which I was concerned.

I could visit an antique and dilapidated dam. There was nothing I could do for it, but it made a wonderful picnic place, with its high rock wall overlooking a deep pool of captive water, and I could strip and plunge and swim beneath a canopy of palm-fronds and lie luxuriating in the cool shade and write a report about it the next morning. There were funds, and a local committee, devoted to the upkeep of these structures, and my own duties were nominal. The important thing was that I should be seen to take an interest.

I could visit a new school. We were perpetually building schools in those days. Although I knew nothing about educa-

K

tion and less about building, I administered the money for these excellent schemes, and it was a constant and reliable entertainment to watch the Hadhramaut builders and architects constructing their elaborate works, pillared and turreted, plastered like wedding-cakes, splendid as Blenheim—and all built of mud.

℞: several dozen donkey-loads of dry earth: a camel-back or two of straw. Add water. Knead well with the feet to make a porridgy paste, spread paste two inches thick on the ground, slice it with a wooden board into twelve-inch squares and leave to dry. The result: bricks.

Meanwhile the ground-plan, sketched by the client on a rough scrap of paper, has been transferred to the building site by means of pegs and stretched string. Two-foot trenches are hacked between the guide-lines by men with mattocks, and filled in with chips of stone bound with cement.

When the foundations have risen a few inches above ground level, the bricks—by now hard and firm—are brought along on coolies' heads from the stooks where they have been baking in the sun. Stuck together with mud and levelled by the same useful pieces of string, the brick courses go up until the foreman thinks the walls are high enough, leaving holes here and there for doors and windows. Hadhramaut builders have been known to forget one of these until the ceiling is ready to go on. No matter: a few pokes with a crow-bar, a few slaps of mud, and all is well. Lintels? Two or three split palm-logs or thorn branches, with grass and twigs stuffed in between to stop the upper layers of brick crumbling through.

For the ceiling, the same material serves: logs or timbers laid across from wall to wall, close together, and wadded with various bits and pieces of vegetation. If pillars have been indicated, by blobs or dots on the scribbled plan, all we require is a few dozen lumps of rock from the base of the cliff, a mason's hammer, and a mason. Chipped into drums, piled one upon the other, pointed with cement, they will stand like the columns of the Parthenon.

Building up from the simple rectangular plan, it is generally easiest to proceed by a system of diminution. For the first storey, delete the corners, leaving a cross-shaped superstructure and four square balconies. For the second floor cut off the arms of the cross, leaving another but smaller replica of the ground floor. And so on: this process can be repeated until the top of the pile is a small central turret.

But so far the future palace (or school) is merely a rough hollow cake of dried earth. For the icing we need a pile of chipped limestone from the cliff-side, a kiln well-stoked with straw and palm-trunks, and a modicum of sugar. We burn the limestone, take it out of the kiln, lay it in the sun and bash it with massy clubs. We mix the pulverised lime with water and smear it on to the outside of the building, several layers thick. It looks like plaster of Paris.

Now comes our master-stroke. Using just the right proportion of sugar, and probably one or two secret ingredients of our own if we are *cordons bleus*, we concoct a plaster which is diamond hard and glaring snow-white. We spread this resplendent preparation throughout the inside, on walls, floors and ceiling; we paint it thick on the crude stone pillars, transforming them into sheer marble columns; and then we take in our practised hand a large round pebble and rub it all over, like a Guardsman boning his boots, to produce a surface of pure porcelain. If we now hire an artist we can have the glittering interior picked out in pink, blue and gold, like the Sultan's Summer Palace, whirling tendrils and bursting buds all over the place; and if we employ a specialist in decorative confectionery he will fashion knops and coigns, balustrades and finials, all from this same plaster, until the whole thing resembles a mad millionaire's dream-house—which is precisely what some of them are.

Much of the Hadhramaut has carried this architectural glorification to a second remove. For the founders of the fortunes were merchant adventurers: in Malaya, in the isles of the East; and they built their town mansions at home with a magnificent disregard for both expense and good taste. In Tarim and Sayun the interested traveller can see reproductions of Rangoon railway stations, of Batavia banking houses, of Penang public libraries . . . all painted and garnished in riotous flourishes, hideously lit by red and blue stained glass—and all made of mud.

The first horseless carriages were chugging around in the Hadhramaut years before there was any road into the valley. The earliest relics are Rugbys: the Rugby Company was liquidated about 1925. The richest of a family of grossly rich old men ordered one of the new-fangled machines some time in the early 1930's. The story goes that he spotted a Pontiac in a Sears Roebuck catalogue and fancied it. The scarlet monster duly arrived at Mukalla, in several pieces; was loaded on a train of camels; hoisted up and over the plateau and deposited at the pioneer motorist's door in Tarim. There it was assembled by a Mukalla mechanic brought in for the job, and it spent the next thirty years conveying its master sedately from his palace to the mosque once every week, on a Friday. When I was in Sayun the old veteran could still be seen, in prime condition, with one or two thousand miles on the clock after thirty years of Friday-go-to-meetings—for after its astonished arrival in that remote crack in the earth's surface there was nowhere else it could go.

But the Automobile Age had dawned in the Hadhramaut; and the next step was inevitable. A road must be built, all the way from Mukalla to Tarim. The grand old man pushed his hand into his ample pocket, counted out several thousand pounds, and invited artisans of unusual talents and uncommon courage to build him a road. In those days the Peace of Ingrams had not yet descended upon the area; so although the engineering project itself was gigantic, most of the money would be needed to buy a way through the several blue-painted tribes who lurked and scuttled like foxes among the rocks of the table-land, and to sweeten the sour faces of the camel-men whose livelihood depended precisely upon there being no alternative means of transport.

Physically, the candidate road-builder faced such a task that if he had in fact been a road-builder he would probably have laughed at it as hopeless at any price. The track had to shin up a thousand feet of cliff wall, grope its way over the plateau, which is no level plain but is scoured and scored with an intricate pattern of ravines, and then topple down about four thousand feet of mountain to the sea.

However, the man who finally took up the challenge was no road-builder. He was a mason; but a mason of such remarkable skill, of so flexible a talent, and so successful in all that he undertook, that he was known as Obeid al Ingliz: English Obeid: as though, in those distant days, no more exalted title could be bestowed upon the master-craftsman of the age.

English Obeid made no time-wasting surveys. Gathering about him a gang of fellow-masons such as I had got to know well at Sanau and Al Abr, cheerful broad-grinning dusky men with large knuckly hands, he made camp at the foot of the cliff and then began methodically to zig-zag up it. None of the team had ever so much as seen a motor road before, but they had seen the famous Pontiac, and gauged as best they could the difference between its track and turning circle and those of a camel. They built up a parapet of boulders jutting out from the precipice, they filled in the gap with small stones and earth, stamping it down hard and firm with their feet; and so they wound their incredible way up the wall of the Hadhramaut.

Over the top was easier; they had camel-paths to follow between the ravines; but every few miles they must stop, sit down, and bargain for some days with one and then another of a succession of grasping hillman clans. When the money ran out, Obeid went back to Tarim and asked the rich old man for more. When he reached the far edge of the plateau—and one can almost hear him shouting, like Xenophon's men, " The sea! The sea!"—he stepped his way down it, trailing his marvellous ribbon behind him, and drew the road triumphantly into Mukalla.

This extraordinary road is still today the main highway for the Hadhramaut, carrying dozens of lorries and smaller vehicles daily up and down, to and fro. But nowadays there is a second road, built in just the same way by Obeid and his nephew—a chip off the old block called English Said. In my day Obeid had been long with his fathers, and Said wore his mantle.

The first time I drove from Mukalla along one of these thoroughfares I nearly went straight over the edge. You bowl along the windy table-top at an easy speed, the ribbon unwinding towards you, and then all of a sudden there is no road in front—alarmed, you slow down—then even more suddenly the whole plateau yawns enormously at your front wheels. You stop. You have to walk to the very edge to see the bottom; and there, far below, are birds wheeling in the clear air, and far below the birds lies a rich green valley, studded with castellated towns. And plunging unhesitatingly over the edge into space is the road, cork-screwing crazily down into the abyss.

When I took over the development schemes in the Hadhramaut I found my most intriguing task was to make a road from Tarim to beyond Shibam, hitherto a torturing buttock-bruising drive through stifling dust between a jigsaw of date-groves and over interminable hump-backed water-channels.

I was delighted at two aspects of this chore. For one, all the donkey-work had been done before: estimates calculated, gangs recruited, lorries obtained, and indeed a few hundred yards of the trackway had been laid at each end.

And secondly, I had Said al Ingliz as chief of staff.

Said was a great man: less great only than his uncle. Built like a bull, he spoke with the deep slow soft voice of a gentle giant. His sinewy arms hung low, suspending huge hands of knotted steel rope. When they held mine in greeting they felt like the jaws of a playful crocodile. Together we drove off to inspect the start of the autobahn.

Said had developed his own technique of road-laying. In the early days of post-war famine-relief the convoys of grain lorries ploughed yard-deep furrows in their tracks, which quickly filled with volatile dust and became rivulets of powder in dry weather and trenches of mud in the wet. Some genius tried clotting the ruts with loose stones. The wheels compressed the gravel, and the result was a sort of compacted ballast railway. Said seized upon this crude germ of an idea and exploited it, with his own peculiar mixture of skills, to produce a system of cobbles like European pavé—but unlike pavé, Said's road surfaces were smooth as tarmac, unruffled by the smallest ripple.

Said mustered, trained, and deployed his team like a general. Under him were two subaltern masons, one in charge of each end of the road, who strode among the labourers imperiously rejecting the smallest deviation from the standards of the master, picking out a mis-placed stone here, checking with a spirit-level there. The road unrolled behind an advancing phalanx of squatting artisans, each one armed with his sharp-nosed hammer, fed with stones by a boy with a basket, judging, measuring, chipping until each grapefruit-sized chunk of rock fitted as exactly into place as a piece of marble inlay.

The well-drilled rank moved methodically forward between the marker cairns, keeping perfect line, and behind them the dead-straight strip of pavement emerged like toothpaste from a tube. A liberal smear of mud followed by a thick sprinkling of gravel, rolled firm by the trucks of the team, finished the job.

There were plenty of problems. One particularly tedious feature of the old route was the long undulation of water-channels, raised four or five feet above ground level, which the track negotiated in the manner of a switchback. Even Said scratched his head over these. Clearly we could tolerate no such humps astride our motorway. Nor could we suggest to the farmers that they might re-route their waterworks: the wells were on one side of the road, the fields on the other. I suggested syphons, and was blinked at by the uncomprehending Said. But I had only to sketch the outline of my idea in the dust with a stick, and he was away to translate my vague wisp of a notion into practical engineering terms. One night when the pumps were silent and no water flowed he calmly cut through the bank of one of the conduits. He buried a length of asbestos piping beneath the level of the roadway. He fashioned a beautiful cement cistern for the water to run down into the pipe from the channel on one side, and a companion shaft for it to rise again on the other. He filled in the trench, patched up the sides, and when the unknowing farmer switched on his pump in the morning he found his stream in magical transit across an eighteen-foot gap. The thing worked; and soon every one of those damnable humps was eagerly sliced away and replaced by our syphons.

Be it said at once that as Uncle Obeid had been no road-builder, merely a genius at improvisation, no more was his nephew Said an engineer, but merely a mason with a gift for solving strange problems. And it must also be said that I was even less of an engineer than I was a mason. Together we approached these obstacles, and somehow we scraped our way over or under or through them.

The biggest challenge of all was a river. Whenever rain falls on the plateau the water floods down into the Hadhramaut through a thousand side ravines and boils along a great gully in the valley floor. For most of the year this river-bed is all dry sand above Tarim; but in spate it is a roaring monster. Said and I looked at it one day and wondered how we were going to cross it—for our new motorway must be cut by no floods, however seasonal or fierce.

One thing we agreed at once. We could not build a bridge. Even if we had the money (and I had to watch the estimates), there was no firm bottom under the silt on which to base the piers—not for sixty or seventy feet. The flood when it came could shift the silt of the bed, and carry the piers and the bridge along with it, if only for a few inches.

Some long-forgotten residue of memory percolated to the surface of my mind. I had heard somewhere of a bridge built *under* a river of this kind—called, for its paradoxical nature, an Irish bridge. If the top of the roadway is laid level with the sand, and if it is adequately anchored by weighty concrete legs rammed into the stuff of the river-bed, then with a sloping ramp at each end cars can cross without slackening speed in the ten dry months of the year; and when the flood comes down it passes harmlessly over the top of the road, which snuggles securely protected in its thick blanket of mud while the torrent rages overhead. Except in the fullest fury of the spate, the place becomes merely a ford. And afterwards all it needs is a squad of men with shovels to scrape it clean.

Said al Ingliz seized with zest upon this mad idea and promptly began to realise it. The next time I visited this part of the route I found an army of labourers; a clanking cement-mixer; an array of deep pits across the river; several heaps of steel wire for reinforcing the concrete framework, so that it might sway before the deluge without snapping.

Soon the clean grey strip of masonry was dipping down, across, and up the other side, with the great bridge invisible beneath the sand. And soon after that came the first flood. We held our breath, Said and I, seemingly for days, until the rain stopped and we could go and see. Said took my hand in his hydraulic press of a paw and shook it silently. The road was still there: muddy but unbowed: damp, but manifestly undrowned.

I hope it has lasted, for Said's sake. It was a work of art.

The European colony in the Hadhramaut was small. There was myself; a bank manager—striving like Hercules to persuade the wealthy Arabs to trust his bank; my assistant, an invaluable young man with a string-thin body and a monkish dedication to his assistant assistant advisership; and one of that close-knit race of peripatetic Scotsmen whose members are found throughout the world in ships' engine-rooms, Army M.I. rooms, and Presbyterian missions. Sid Morrison made the nearest approach he could to a ship's engine-room: he ran a workshop for the twelve hundred diesel pumps which irrigated the valley. Sid had a round red face and convivial ways, like so many of his breed, and his silver-haired motherly wife was the only representative of her sex among us. But that was our lot: three bachelors, and Mr. and Mrs. Sid. There were other satellites of the Residency: a lean eager Co-operative man; a plump, self-assertive Agricultural man; but both were Arabs. There was a rangy mustard-coloured Indian doctor. Later came three or four crew-cut American oil men, but they never stayed long.

So social life in the Hadhramaut was meagre; and outlets for extraverts nil. But occasionally my life was enlivened by a

visitor from abroad—like Dr. Ritz (as I had better call him),
a lofty European politician, with as much tact as a cart-horse.
He was on his way to South Africa for some purpose of State
and elected to stop over in the Hadhramaut *en route*—or off
route—to see the sights made famous by Freya Stark. He
stayed with me. He had elegant silver hair and the sort of
noble, handsome, but strangely unattractive face that Dag
Hammarskjoeld wore.

The august Doctor was an excruciating embarrassment.

Speaking no Arabic, Dr. Ritz used me as interpreter. If he
had committed his gaffes in person it would have been painful;
but as nobody heard him drop them, and the audience only
received the pearls of gaucherie from the lips of their Assistant
Adviser, it was exquisite torment for me. He made sly risqué
remarks about the female sex, to a long-bearded gathering
of descendants of the Prophet; when I demurred, he nudged
me in the ribs, until with eyes raised heavenwards I stuttered
out the joke which by now was as stale as bile in my mouth.
If I had been quicker-witted I could have ad-libbed some
pleasantry about the date-harvest; but my mind, numbed by
the crassness of it all, merely acted as a translating machine.
Introduced to the representative of the Mukalla Sultan in
Shibam, Dr. Ritz gravely lectured that astonished gentleman
on the merits of federation. In the political context of those
days it was like tendering the same counsel to Kenneth
Kaunda and Hastings Banda in 1960. If Dr. Ritz had said
it himself, the Sayid would merely have shrugged him off as
an interfering outsider. But it was my lips, my tongue, that
had to force their way around the outrageous syllables. . . .
The Doctor chose to deliver a short but didactic lecture on
early Arab history, with particular reference to the Hadhramaut, in the presence of the actual historian of the Hadhramaut, contradicting with such patience, such patronising
kindness in his rôle of bearer of the torch of enlightenment
that I could only stretch my eyes covertly at the incredulous
historian, imploring his forgiveness.

Another delightful diversion was the arrival, every few

weeks, of a plane-load of Americans. These beings were global packaged tourists whose enterprising agency had arranged a day trip to the Fabulous Land of Incense, the Sensational Valley of Hadhramaut, to beguile the dreary hours of refuelling in Aden. A regular feature of their itinerary was a Banquet with a Genuine Sultan.

The Sultan, bless his good heart, invited all his distinguished visitors to lunch, to welcome them, after the immemorial custom of Arab hospitality. That was the occasion as he saw it. But the tourists saw it merely as a way of stuffing their movie cameras with something their neighbours back home hadn't got. I was supposed to be there, too: the Sultan thought I might like a good lunch while it was going: but the idea of appearing on several dozen home movie screens in Milwaukee and Kansas City as a Genuine British Colonial Officer dried up my appetite fast.

Few of the dollar princes and princesses made even an attempt to taste the certainly gorgeous feast the Sultan put on for them. They did not even sit down. They gorged, instead, on movie shots of His Highness, of roast sheep, of mounds of spiced rice, of barefoot black servitors; and having filled the bellies of their cameras to burping point, they wanted to go and fix themselves some chow someplace. I myself never even saw them: I hope they are disappointed at that.

FOURTEEN

The Last of the Gunboats

GUNBOAT—a richly evocative word, calling forth brilliant images of the benevolent exercise of imperial power under the hot tropic sun. Whether such a vessel ever existed, in strict naval parlance, is known only to naval men. But it has steamed triumphantly into the mythology of Empire, where it now floats serene as the very epitome of global dominion.

So when Arthur Watts and his superiors in Aden had run their full nine months' course of cogitation and intrigue, and ultimately brought forth a plan for the unilateral solution of the Mahra problem, they called their brain-child " Operation Gunboat ". For my well-meant attempts to win over those wild people by liberality and eloquence had yielded no fruit. The standing obstacles were still unsurmounted: their distrust of the Sultan; their distrust of the colonial Government (the Mahra were wholly incapable of believing that the Government's intentions were disinterested and merely fatherly); hatred and jealousy of each other, focused now especially upon those like Bin Hezhaz and the Sanau clique who collaborated with us; a genuine appreciation of the virtues of their own way of life, anarchy tempered by vendetta; and withal, a deep yearning for better things.

The Mahra nation was a shy virgin bride. Treasuring their maidenhood, yet longing inwardly for the delights in store, they were psychologically unable to bring themselves to embrace their benefactor, to invite his drastic penetration.

They lay there, passive, challenging the Government to ravish them—fingernails bared to resist the secretly welcome assault.

Faced with this quite understandable attitude, once it had become apparent, the authorities took the only course they could. They purchased half a dozen armoured scout cars, a fleet of troop-carrying lorries, and a complementary quantity of weapons. Pat Gray enrolled two hundred extra men into the Hadhrami Bedouin Legion. The Royal Air Force was asked to provide a four-engined bomber. And the Rape of the Mahra was on.

The last gunboat in British imperial history was about to be launched: Captain, Colonel Eric Johnson; First Officer, Pat Gray; Chief Mate (civil affairs), myself, withdrawn from Sayun for the cruise.

Eric Johnson was the man for the job. He bore the title of Military Assistant to the Resident Adviser and British Agent. He was a sort of floating Chief of Staff, with no direct responsibility of command but with a brief to advise the R.A. upon matters military throughout the Protectorate. These were complicated. The Bedouin Legion was the R.A.'s own mailed fist, but the Sultans had their knuckles too, in bemusing confusion. There was the Kathiri Army, under Captain Saleh, whom I had met and admired in Sayun; there were also Kathiri Police. The Mukalla Sultan had a regular army, an armed constabulary, and some more police. There were several sorts of customs guards and other enlisted bodies of men. The Kathiri Sultan even owned his own corps of militant slaves. All these fanatically independent bands wore different coloured hats—and most of them were Eric Johnson's pidgin. Shortly before I first arrived in the Protectorate, one of the tribes near Mukalla had staged a serious and murderous rebellion, and all the motley armed resources of the Hadhramaut were mobilised to stamp it out. Eric Johnson commanded this operation, deploying and manoeuvring his miscellaneous troops with extraordinary skill: an unsung feat of generalship.

As I was grateful when I took over Al Abr that I had known Pat Gray, so I was thankful now that I had once soldiered under Johnson. He had been my C.O. nine years before when we had raised and trained the nucleus of what were to become the Trucial Oman Scouts. He was a difficult man to serve. Lean and rigid as a pikestaff, armed with a razor-edged tongue, he maintained a personal professional standard of almost Prussian perfection—and expected it of others. Recluse and ascetic to the point of eccentricity he made it his habit to sleep on the ground with his men on campaign, to share their rice, to seek their company in preference to that of his own kind. He was a hard and polished weapon of war.

I was the odd man out—a civilian on a grimly military enterprise. Between Johnson and Gray the relationship was clear, the established bond between a commander and his lieutenant. But I was like a raw commissar with Voroshilov, a youthful chaplain with Pizarro. I had my own responsibility, as I saw it: to fulfil the pledge I had given the Mahra a year ago, that the Government which they feared would never warrant their fears. I was determined that the invasion of Mahra should be bloodless, and preferably shotless. The grand old warrior Gray was not my problem. My political attachment was to Johnson, that stiff military man.

I was glad that I had known him before.

So once more, and for the last time, I loaded my Land-Rover with a box of tin kitchen kit, a case of whisky, lots of tea and tunny and rice, rolls of bedding and Hassan the cook. Anticipating awkwardness, I carefully folded my priceless firman from Socotra and put it in my breast pocket. Leaving my thin keen deputy in charge of the Hadhramaut, and taking a last look at the cool tank of water in the comfortable white house, I drove north to the desert.

While the armada was assembling at Thamud, where Pat Gray and Eric Johnson were mustering and marshalling, inspecting and provisioning, I had my own force to recruit and embody. The more Mahra tribesmen I could beguile into joining Gunboat, and the more tribes they represented, the easier my task was going to be. The riddle was, how to inveigle the

Mahra into becoming accessories to the invasion of their own country.

I had two short days for the job. Signals had bleeped to Sanau and Habarut, calling some of the more useful local leaders to meet me to discuss a matter of mutual concern. The whole desert—indeed the whole Protectorate—knew something was up: the political prods over the past year, and the impressive military parade now falling in at Thamud, could hardly be disguised. Some feeble cover story was put about to account for the massive build-up, but on the whole, opinion among the tribes seemed divided between ridiculing the very idea that the ailing British lion would now dare to make a last imperial pounce, and asking what else that animal could conceivably be going to do. At any rate, curiosity and avarice combined to bring my guests hurrying into the two forts, and when I reached Sanau I at once sent off a truck to bring Bin Hezhaz and a couple of friends from Habarut.

Conspicuous at Sanau was Sulayim bin Domaish. There too, were Ashayer, Bashayer, Bin Woraiga, and many other Wadi Mahrat comrades. Agog with excitement they crowded into my upper room in the fort and waited—peculiarly quiet—for me to tell them what was afoot.

Wasting no time, I told them—baldly. " The Government is going to Ghaidha," I said.

They nodded, as if they had known it all along.

" I want you to come with us."

More nods, but cautious now.

Then Sulayim asked: " How many companies have you got, Assistant Adviser?"

The company was the largest military unit the Bedouin could comprehend. All the garrisons of Thamud, Sanau, and Habarut comprised one company.

" Four."

The heads wagged, more assured.

" And eight tanks." The distinction between scout car and tank was too fine for the Mahra.

One or two began gingerly to smile.

" And an aeroplane—with machine-guns and bombs."

And now they settled back, happy. Their tribal pride could never allow them to confess that mere soldiers, even by the thousand, would overawe or even alarm their stout-hearted fellow-Mahra. But " tanks ", and above all an aeroplane, pushed up the stakes. They were like a nuclear threat. They would give the heartland Mahra a face-saving excuse not to put up too much of a fight.

It only remained for me to explain, at their request, just why the good British were doing this rude and out-dated thing. " Your Sultan," I said, " is coming to Ghaidha to meet his subjects." It was not really a lie. The man had been invited, though none of us believed for a moment that he would dare to come. " We are going there to mount a guard of honour, commensurate with his prestige as Sultan of Mahra. I am inviting you to ride with the convoy, to save you the trouble of going all the way to Ghaidha by camel—besides, you might be too late."

This piece of blarney was good enough. The Mahra knew it was rubbish, but it enabled them to pretend to themselves and each other that it was, after all, merely a guard of honour and not a blitzkrieg. Anxious not to be left out of an enterprise which offered them vistas of glory—" surely," I said, " you would want to be among the first to usher in this new age for your people "—they agreed. They muttered muffled protests when I said we were off that very evening (leaving no time for any hot-footed cameleer to spread the news), but they accepted it, perceiving the reason for my haste.

Bin Hezhaz arrived, with his couple of friends, and I treated them to the same spiel. The wise chieftain of Habarut had guessed it all, and I had no difficulty persuading him to join us.

Then, when all was quiet that evening and I was making ready for the move, Sulayim shuffled back in. He led a stranger by the hand, a shifty-eyed man with a black spade beard and too many teeth in his mouth.

" This gentleman would like a lift to Ghaidha," said Sulayim, innocent as a boy scout.

It was like a stray Trojan asking for a lift back home in

the Wooden Horse. My immediate impulse was to lock the toothy hitch-hiker up in the fort, incommunicado; and Sulayim too, for blabbing. But reason intervened. The fastest camel, if it had set off as soon as my purpose had been published, could not reach the water-shed before the motor column. And besides, the fellow wanted to come *with* us—

" Who is he?" I asked, no more penetrating question occurring to me.

" Salem is his name," Sulayim said. Then after a small pause, and with a sidelong half-wink : " Salem Qamsiti."

Qamsiti. The Qamsit were one of the obscurer but more vicious tribes of the Mahra, with whom we had no contact at all. And they lived below Jebel Fart—just where we would cross the invisible line from Manahil to Mahra land. The dire Qamsit might well be the first warriors to welcome us as we barged through their door. If so, I would need a man from the Qamsit . . . . I despatched Salem Qamsiti to collect his luggage and join the other fellow-travellers.

I held Sulayim back. " Whose idea was this?" I asked him, as casually as I could.

Sulayim pulled out his brass cigarette and filled it and lit it with a match I gave him.

" I thought he might come in useful, Assistant Adviser," he said, as if talking about a map or a spare pair of shoes. " We have no guides from south of the watershed, and we shall have to pick them up as we go. It is best to have one with us first, before the trouble can start."

" Guides," of course, meant companions—men upon whose faces I would be. The great armoured convoy was a far more comforting sort of escort, but if my ambition of a peaceful penetration was to be realised, I needed faces as much as guns.

A thought struck me. " Does Salem Qamsiti really want a lift to Ghaidha?"

The pursed lips crinkled into the familiar chilling smile. " He does now," said Sulayim.

I mused for a few moments, upon Sulayim's limpid foresight, his firm initiative, his obviously uncanny powers of persuasion. I remembered his performance at that meeting with

L

Al Nissi, and several similar *tours de force* before and since, most of which had been directed against the British Government. I suddenly saw a dreadful vision of the damage Sulayim could wreak upon our venture, the utter havoc he could cause, by a mere flicker of an eyebrow, a soft word slipping from his lips, which could completely misrepresent our purpose and turn all the tribes irrevocably against us. Since Sulayim must come, it was better that he came securely bound to the Gunboat's bowsprit.

Sulayim sat on, smoking placidly.

I cast the die.

"Sulayim, Her Majesty's Government offers you some work."

He shrugged. "I need no work, Assistant Adviser. I do well enough, here and there, with this and that. . . ."

I bet you do, I thought. But—"Work like Tomatum's."

Tomatum's pay, prestige, and perquisites were objects almost of scandal throughout the Protectorate. Sulayim raised an eyebrow as a token of interest aroused.

"You accept?"

"I am deeply honoured."

Relieved, I made my second throw. "But your fellow Mahra will be jealous, will they not?"

"The Mahra are a jealous people, Assistant Adviser."

I knew that Sulayim, once exposed as a stipendiary British stooge among the Mahra, would be like Samson without his hair. And the only way he could then regain his former ascendancy would be to double-cross us: a thing he would do with skill and alacrity. So—"Sulayim, this must be a secret."

A ghost of a chuckle flickered around the tight sphincter of his mouth.

"Because of this jealousy of the Mahra, we must keep our agreement strictly between ourselves. Only you and I know of this. If I hear one word about your job from any other tongue but yours, I shall know that you have been spilling the secret, for I shall know it was not me. And that will cancel your appointment—and your pay." I paused. "And if you let us down, I'll tell your friends that you have sold out to us."

Sulayim was unperturbed. "In the name of God," he said, and he shuffled up and rustled out like a caricature of Rasputin. As I regarded his retreating back I thought: My secret weapon. And if it blows up in my face I have nobody to blame but myself.

That night I drove out of Sanau to the rendezvous with the military south of Thamud. With me rode the Mahra, prominent amongst whom were Sulayim bin Domaish and Salem Qamsiti.

At daybreak the armada arrived. Eric Johnson took the lead, with Doghash, his favourite Desert Guard, beside him. I followed, with Sulayim and the Qamsiti. Two armoured scout cars ranged behind us, and the rest of the convoy— Pat Gray's whiskers like a banner—fell into line behind. We drove through the whole of the next day, down the track Tomatum had showed me the year before and which Johnson had since reconnoitred in detail, and we camped on the second evening below the towering pink prow of Jebel Fart, on the very brink of the Mahra homeland. There the soldiers were harangued, issued with field dressings, and stood down anxiously to rest, fully expecting a major battle on the morrow. Johnson walked among their fires, chatting here and there like Henry V before Agincourt, giving his men "a little touch of Eric in the night."

I was scared stiff. My only comfort was Salem Qamsiti, who assured me that if he was loaded conspicuously on to the front vehicle we need have no worries: "all the Qamsit are my friends," he declared. "The Bait Suhail too. If they but see my beard"—and he stroked the splendid growth with pride—"they will know that Salem is with you, and they will be your friends too. *As long as I am the first man they see.*"

But Johnson would hear none of it. He must lead, as was his right and his duty. And he would have no strange Bedouin, Qamsit or otherwise, in his vehicle. Doghash was his right hand and he needed and wanted no other. The best I could do was to pile the poor fellow on top of a three-ton lorry which would travel immediately behind the two armoured cars backing up the colonel. I had been relegated to a post further down the column for the forthcoming encounter.

The nervous dawn came up with a rush. Johnson made military dispositions: vanguard, advance guard, flank guards, rearguard. Feeling like the Grand Army crossing the Niemen we churned up the dust and ground noisily off—past the foot of Jebel Fart—over the border and into the forbidden land.

Soon the wide grey gravel plain began to break up into rills, then gullies, then deep channels, as the terrain dipped into the basin of the great trunk river, the Jizza. Lining our left flank stretched the endless pink precipice. The vehicles wound and twisted through narrow valleys dotted with stunted thorn trees, clambered up and over shingly ridges between the veins of the eroded slopes. The going was cramped but not difficult. I cast anxious eyes at the skyline as we negotiated the troughs, wishing that my Qamsiti was sitting on the bonnet of the front truck—

Suddenly we had stopped. Lorries lurched desperately to cover, khaki figures flowed in floods over the sides and scuttled up the slopes. My Legion driver, well-trained, burrowed his Land-Rover into a cluster of boulders. I edged gingerly up a rise and saw below me the vanguard halted higgledy-piggledy in a soldier's nightmare of a defile. I heard no shooting; but ranged like stone saints along a cathedral cornice, a party of Bedouin was lining the heights above the ravine. For a moment the scene was a stopped motion-picture—soldiers frozen in the act of scrambling uphill, trucks crystallised in a crazy scattered pattern, the Mahra sentinels erect and still on the skyline. What a place, I thought, to be halted—within half an hour of launching our boat!

A messenger was shouting up at me. " Colonel wants you," he trumpeted. I slid down the stones and into my Land-Rover and drove frightenedly past the petrified column to the front, where I found Eric Johnson drinking tea under a tree and marvelled at his coolness and the efficiency of his servant.

" Somebody up there is asking for you," said the colonel, between sips. " You'd better go and see what he wants."

I gibbered slightly, then over my shoulder I caught a

glimpse of an anguished-looking black beard trying to hoist itself off a lorry fifty yards back. Salem Qamsiti dropped over
the side like a chunk of jetsam and sprinted up to me. " I told
you so!" he wailed. " What could I do, back there?"

" Are these Qamsit?" I snapped at him, as I walked reluctantly forward to meet a stately figure in smart white clothes
which was stepping down the hill in front.

" Not Qamsit," puffed Salem, " but our cousins—Bait
Suhail."

I shook my head irritably, squinting at the white-robed
apparition now striding steadily towards me.

Suddenly it spoke. And the only way I can convey the
meaning and the inflection of its outburst is by translating
thus : " What the hell do you think you're doing?"

It was a voice I knew; and as we drew close I saw beneath
the shining rainbow-hued head-dress a pair of furiously frowning eyes, a navy-blue face stretched taut as a drum-skin, a grin
like the death-throes of tetanus.

It was Saleh bin Matiaa : dressed to kill.

FIFTEEN

Tug-of-War in Mahra Land

"WHAT the blazes are you playing at, barging through my country like this?"

We were sat under a thorn tree, Saleh and I, with the Qamsiti in attendance. I was receiving an imperial dressing-down.

"You, of all people, ought to know better!" Saleh acted more sorrowful than angry. "You don't go breaking into people's homes with an army, without even telling them you're coming! Suppose we'd opened fire. The whole of the Mahra nation between here and the sea would have flown to arms. Why didn't you tell me first? There's a right way and a wrong way, and you've gone about it the wrong way."

I was blistered. There had of course been no possible way of preparing him, without sacrificing the speed and the security which was our main protection. But he had a point, and he pressed it home, in terms which I can only paraphrase—so spit-splattered was his bluster and so garbled his speech.

I had been lucky to be a friend of Pat Gray; I was fortunate to have served under Eric Johnson. But never before or since have I been so glad that I knew somebody. Saleh bin Matiaa and his Bait Suhail, posted with considerable tactical skill astride the first serious defile on our line of march, could have lamed the enterprise: with perhaps a harmful delay for a battle, the tribes downstream alerted, and above all the incalculable damage which a fight, however victorious, would have wrought upon the name of the newly-launched Gun-boat.

Saleh went on fuming, and out of the corner of my eye I saw the colonel waxing restive at the tedious hold-up. He kept sending small scraps of paper with curt messages on them: " What's going on?" " We can't stay here all day!" " I'm leaving in ten minutes ". But if we were to proceed with comfort through the country ahead I must pacify Bin Matiaa, and through him his fire-bellied tribesmen who thought they saw a helpless column of soldiers wallowing at their mercy and were blissfully ignorant of the main bulk of the force at Johnson's disposal, round the corner.

The dialogue droned on; the irritable memos proliferated. And at last a mollified Bin Matiaa agreed to come with us to Ghaidha, in order not to be thought backward in the ushering in of the new age of the Mahra. Bin Matiaa insisted on riding in the front, as Salem Qamsiti had demanded before, so that he could forestall any more misunderstandings. And this time Johnson agreed to carry a local " guide " in his cab. And this time, too, he put me to travel in second place, with the armoured cars at the back of me and the soldiers of the van-guard behind them.

So off we went merrily through the land of the Qamsit and Bait Suhail. The only audible complaints issued from Saleh bin Matiaa, who suffered sorely from car-sickness and spent the rest of the day with a green tinge glimmering through his woad groaning and retching over the side of the disgusted colonel's Land-Rover.

The rest of that day's progress developed into a tug-of-war between Johnson and me.

The colonel, on whose shoulders lay the most appalling weight of responsibility, saw one safe way to reach Ghaidha—to slice like a knife through the empty land before the Mahra had time to assemble at the danger spots. The Mahra, even more than Arab Bedouin, can gather in hordes from out of empty space with terrifying speed at the sound of a shot or the call of a tribesman. The further we drove into this unseen world the more tiny and alone we felt. We had three hundred miles of completely unknown country to cover, with the alarming prospect of the Mahra capital at the end of the trail. Our fifty trucks, our scout cars, our four hundred soldiers seemed but an extreme impertinence as we crawled our way through a land the size of Wales inhabited by some tens of thousands of well-armed barbarians. Even our bomber, which by now was growling in circles overhead, once or twice an hour zooming down with a full-throated roar twenty feet overhead to encourage our men and stampede lurking ambushers, was a moral rather than a practical weapon. And there was nothing behind us at all. There was no question of a relief column. If we ran into a severe physical obstacle, and were bogged down long enough for the Mahra to muster in strength, no Havelock, no Colin Campbell would come with pipes a-skirling to cut us out. We learnt after it was all over that hostile Mahra, more than once, had approached the soldiers of the escort asking, in effect, why they as Muslims were doing this ill-mannered thing, and inviting them to surrender the Christians who were the cause of it all and go home in peace. The soldiers told the Mahra to wash their mouths out. But if the force had really been in trouble, we few infidels might have found ourselves jettisoned.

So I envied the colonel none of his anxiety, and I grudged him none of his urgent haste. But whenever we encountered Mahra along the way, invariably they shot at us, attracting their fellows like a magnet, and I had no choice but to halt and send out the " guides " to parley with the *franc tireurs* while Johnson champed and chafed at the bit and pawed the ground. Once he drove on without me, leaving me and Salem Qamsiti still arguing desperately with a trio of incredibly obstinate Qamsit, whom we were frightened to leave in midspeech for fear of aggravating their mood. Luckily we managed to entice them to come with us—in the hope of a *pourboire*—and we raced to catch up the convoy before any more Qamsit arrived.

At times, indeed, the army advanced like a leech: the head pressing on, the middle and tail stuck behind, till the wormlike column was stretched to twice its normal length. Then with a quick scuttle the hindparts caught up with the front, which by then had been halted again.

The countryside opened out for a while into a broad horizon-wide rolling gravel plain, which deceived us into hoping it was all going to be like that to Ghaidha. Then we dipped over a slope into an astonishingly beautiful river-bed, with a blue flowing stream flanked with clusters of palms and flowering oleanders, lined with great white boulders and chalky-pink cliffs. We were in the Jizza: the highway to Ghaidha. We had, it seemed, but to follow this wide, lazy meander between its low cliff banks a long shot away on either side, to debouch in due course upon the open coastal flats—where Ghaidha should lie at our feet.

So down the Jizza we bowled, feeling strangely light of heart. As evening fell we halted, in a place where a tributary stream oozed down from the left. This was the mouth of the Wadi Mahrat. Here was water in abundance; a spacious bowl for a camp; only three or four nearby knolls and ridges to picquet, and the dark red mountains far out of range around us. Just round the corner of the Mahrat lay Murayt, the village of Daloum, that ancient peace-maker who had attended the Bait Suhail tribunal at Thamud. He was supposed to be friendly.

We were half-way to Ghaidha; with not a shot fired from our side, despite the many fusillades directed at our column throughout the day. Here Pat Gray was to establish a base, holding the half-way house. The sun went down behind a jagged pile of mahogany-coloured peaks, the camp-fires spread their drifting veils of smoke in the still air, and we looked forward to a straight run down the Jizza on the morrow.

It was after supper that Sulayim sidled up to me, leading Salem Qamsiti by the hand. The pair looked perturbed: almost scared. They sat down beside me and mumbled a few exchanges of conventional triviality.

Salem was the first to unburden his mind.

"Are you going on down the Jizza tomorrow, Assistant Adviser?"

I was reminded, creepily, of that evening at Khayas.

" Yes," I said. " Where do you think we're going? "

Salem twitched his head over his shoulder to make sure nobody else was near. " I know a better way," he said.

Sulayim was gazing vacantly at the stars, as though dissociating himself from the Qamsiti's design.

Salem went on to explain. By climbing out of the Jizza a few miles downstream, he whispered, we would find ourselves running along a flat plateau where there was no possibility of successful ambush or obstructive defence. " Broad as the sea," he said. " But if you go down the Jizza. . . ." He left his words hanging eerily in the air.

Here was a dilemma of horrifying size. The maps showed that the Jizza was the only way. Aerial survey had showed no route but the Jizza. The military plan was tied to the Jizza. Eric Johnson had talked for months of nothing but the Jizza. Our next and final tribe, now that we had successfully nipped through the Qamsit and Bait Suhail, were the Kilshat, and the Kilshat were known and feared throughout the whole land as the largest, most powerful, best armed and most ferociously hostile of all that terrifying race. We knew we must pass through the Kilshat. But the Jizza, a rocky river valley devoid of useful vegetation and so presumably deserted, had seemed the perfect and obvious way, even if it was not, as we believed, the only road to the sea. The Kilshat could rush to the hills as they heard us approach, but we would move too fast for them, and would sail grandly down the channel, like the *Scharnhorst* and *Gneisenau* through the Straits of Dover, while the Kilshat gnashed their teeth impotently above and behind us. The Qamsiti's plateau, if it existed, and if we could get there, presumably swarmed with Kilshat.

With my head in a whirl I left Sulayim and Salem and sought out my other friends. Individually, confidentially, I asked each one whether in fact they thought the Jizza was the best, if not the only, way: whether, perhaps, there might not be a better route, say up on the right. And one by one they shrugged their shoulders and said: " God knows. We do not know these parts. This is the land of the Kilshat." Only

Ashayer, that speaker of truth, glancing nervously this way and that, said in normal times the Jizza should be passable but recently there had been heavy floods, and now he wondered. . . .

I crept back to Salem and Sulayim, and questioned them again. Salem was adamant. The Jizza, he said, was a death-trap. Up on the right, we would meet the Kilshat, probably in force, but the ground favoured us. In the Jizza there were— so far—no Kilshat, but there was no road either, and the Kilshat would come soon enough. We could take our choice, said Salem Qamsiti.

I was convinced, and profoundly grateful that Sulayim was earning his clandestine keep. For it was obvious that all our other companions, even Ashayer, were scared witless at the thought of being accused by the Kilshat of guiding the Government through their land. They would see us floundering help-less in the impassable gorge while the Kilshat gathered relentlessly, and trust to God and their own glibness and fleet-ness to extricate themselves, rather than seem to have shown us the only feasible way to Ghaidha. But, I reflected, they had to live in this country after we had all gone.

But now I had to persuade Eric Johnson, with all his other worries, and with his marked maps, his meticulous plans, his entire preconception of the morrow's route: on the word of a casual stranger, against that of his best advisers. His was the grim responsibility. If I was a dupe, and Salem a traitor, we might never get out of Mahra alive. His choice must have been agonising. But in the end he made it.

The next morning we drove out of Pat Gray's camp, leaving a third of our strength behind. We trundled down the Jizza for a few miles—where I had the unnerving accident of a punc-tured tyre, for which the column could not wait, and never has a Land-Rover wheel been changed with such race-track speed—and then we turned sharp right up a side valley, breasted a slope, found ourselves on the lip of a spacious tawny plain sprinkled with green trees reaching without hindrance to the horizon—and promptly came under fire from a knoll to our front.

We had met the Kilshat; within an hour. The Qamsiti's fore-
cast was coming convincingly to pass. The rocky hill before
us was spewing bullets and crawling with men and goats. More
significant, scattered shots were flying down at us from several
hundred yards to our left. These came from an eminence
which very obviously overlooked the Jizza just a short way
below where we had climbed out of the valley. So the Kilshat
had been lying in ambush after all. Their frustration must
have been acute as they watched us calmly walking out of
their trap. Caught in the gorge, even by a handful of snipers,
we would have been more than uncomfortable; here on the
heights we could take cover, deploy, manoeuvre, if necessary
attack.

Once more the vanguard halted and assumed an attitude of
aggressive defence. And once more the colonel reined back
his troops, who were by now boiling with repressed martial
fury. Every time they met the enemy, it seemed, even on
ground so favourable to themselves, that damned Political
Officer must go and chat to the bandits instead of letting the
soldiers get on with their job and teach the Mahra a few
condign lessons. A morale problem was beginning to develop,
and Johnson could sense it. But he was becoming inured to
his pestilent civilian attaché, and he resignedly let me try
again.

On a word from Johnson his guide Doghash raised his
head over a boulder and hailed the Kilshat chief on his hillock.
A weird bird-call echoed back.

" By God," said Doghash. " It's my brother-in-law, Muhsin!" And precipitately he sprang up, and waving his turban
in the traditional gesture of truce he began to lope from stone
to stone towards the hill. His leaping turned at once into a
wild capering dance as bullets thwacked into the ground about
his feet. He dived to earth again, still waving his headcloth
desperately over the cover.

After an anxious moment, when Johnson's wrath at the
peppering of his guide threatened to unleash the straining
legionaries, the fusillade ceased, and cautiously Doghash edged

forward once again, alternately calling out his own name and that of his belligerent brother-in-law. This time his advance was unaccompanied by the whew of lead, though covered closely by a whole company of the Legion, and he trotted, still waving, towards the knoll, which swallowed him up.

We waited for perhaps fifteen minutes before we saw him step down off a ledge full of huddled goats and walk more sedately back to our positions. Another man was with him. The stranger sat down on a boulder when they had reached half-way, and Doghash returned to us alone.

" Muhsin wants to talk to the Assistant Adviser," said Doghash.

I glanced towards the colonel, who wrinkled his thin face in distaste and said: " Tell him to come closer. We won't harm him."

Another prolonged exchange of wild calls ensued. Then Doghash pointed to a small outcrop of rock, about a hundred yards away from our front line, where I was to meet with Muhsin. I rose and made my way edgily out of cover towards the exposed trysting place, where I sat, feeling like a coconut at a fair. But the rules were observed; nobody tried to knock me off; and Muhsin strode across the plain and climbed up to my perch and stood waiting for me to say something.

He was a thick-set man with a grey headcloth and grey clothes and a woolly grey beard like stuffing from a sofa. He wore an imperious air of authority and at the same time a look of injured dignity that made me feel very small. I stood up and offered him " peace ", which with deliberate hesitation he returned. We shook hands, as if we each expected the other to be holding a scorpion in his palm. We settled down and Doghash moved a short way off and turned his back politely on our parley.

" What are you doing?" Muhsin asked me, as a man might who sees a strange army marching through his back garden.

" We are off to Ghaidha," I said, as gaily as I could, " to meet the Sultan."

" Without letting us know?" It was almost a repetition of Saleh bin Matiaa's grumble at Jebel Fart.

" We are telling you now," was the best I could do in reply.
" Why not come along with us and meet your Sultan?"

Muhsin was regal in the face of *force majeure*. " If my
Sultan wants to meet me," he said, " he sends me a message
first. And even our Sultan cannot pass through the land of
the Kilshat without asking our leave, without taking an escort
from our tribe."

" But the Sultan is coming to Ghaidha by ship. We have to
go this way because there is no other road."

" I see. If you want to proceed through our country, you
must do it in the customary way. You must ask our permission
for your journey; and you must take guides from among us."

" I am asking you now for leave, and guides."

" I," said Muhsin, " am not the Kilshat. I am only one of
the fifty chiefs of the Kilshat. To obtain our agreement, you
must stay here at our threshold, while I summon my brethren.
Then we can talk. And if they all agree, you can go through
to Ghaidha, safe from our rifles."

Since such a conference would take at least a week to
convene, and there was not the smallest chance of it being
anything but a bloody riot, even my conciliatory instincts were
overborne by plain logic.

" That is impossible," I told Muhsin. " We have an appointment with the Sultan and we hope to meet all the Kilshat,
indeed all the Mahra, at Ghaidha. We cannot wait here long
enough to talk to them first."

" Then I refuse you permission to travel further."

" Then I am sorry. We would wish for nothing more than
to make our journey with the blessing of the Kilshat."

" That I cannot give you, and I order you back."

" That is your privilege. We, in any case, are going on to
Ghaidha."

The parley had reached an impasse, which we both recognised, and Muhsin stood up to go. His last words were: " I
forbid you." Then without a handshake, without a farewell,
for we were now technically at war, he strode back to his hill.

Honour was satisfied. Muhsin had done all he could: he
had shut his door in our face. If we now forced it open,

with our armoured cars and our thundering bomber, then that was our—and presumably God's—will. We waited till he was safely out of sight among his goats, and then we drove on, unmolested.

We met the Kilshat several times more that day. But we were running to schedule; we hoped to reach Ghaidha by evening; the Qamsiti's route was superb—a huge tree-studded prairie, where the terrain so obviously favoured our mechanised column that most groups of that hot-tempered tribe did no more than stand and stare at us as we rumbled monstrously through their homeland. Now that the Qamsiti had betrayed the way, and was safely left behind at Murayt, Doghash and the other guides showed an intimate knowledge of the country. Once a straggling water-truck broke down and attracted a volley of ill-aimed fire. Hearing the sinister pop-pop-popping from half a mile ahead, the colonel despatched me with a scout car to investigate. I found a sheepish flock of Kilshat youths standing in a tight knot bayed by bare-fanged legionaries—the lieutenant on the spot had acted swiftly and skilfully.

I was anxious to seduce a Kilshati to join our march. Salem and Bin Matiaa had proved their worth when we rubbed up against the Qamsit and the Bait Suhail the day before, but they would have been worse than useless here. So I invited the captured gang to join us; but to nobody's surprise they declined, and we let them go galloping off towards the horizon yelling curses in their secret tongue. The Kilshat were living up to their reputation. They hated the other Mahra, they loathed us, they despised their Sultan. They were an arrogantly powerful tribe whose vengeful temper was patiently storing up this succession of outrages against the day when they would demand a reckoning. This sentiment was discernible throughout the Kilshat chapter: from Muhsin to the youths; a formidable carapace of tribal dignity protecting them from bloody-minded gestures of aggressiveness and mercenary collaboration alike.

Meanwhile Johnson grappled with his own problems, in particular the mood of his troops, who were feeling more and more cheated out of the feat of arms that they had been anticipating ever since stepping across the Rubicon. But I was within reach of my goal, and Johnson was backing me. Not one of the Legion's thousands of rounds had been used against the Mahra, not one rifle-barrel blackened. With blood on our hands we would face the Mahra as conquerors: a difficult guise in which to make friends. With clean hands we could hope, however forlornly, to show that we came to Ghaidha in peace.

I had only one really horrible half-hour. We had left the wide upland behind us and were screwing our way through a shadowy ravine—I remember protesting to Doghash, but he assured us that this passage was short, though unavoidable —when the sickly water truck broke down again. We stopped; we had no choice. While the fitters worked like bees to get the bowser on the road we sat there, Johnson and I together, regarding our column lying lifeless and naked along the chasm. Our eyes were hypnotically drawn to the high banks that pressed down on us like jaws of a huge vice. Every minute that passed was one more without a turbaned head breaking the skyline, without the hideous shuddering cry of the Mahra tally-ho, without the clenched fist on the heart that seems to precede by a split second the crack of a bullet. Here, if anywhere, the truncated Gunboat could have been torpedoed. So narrow was the valley that the vehicles were unable to move, except straight ahead. We were spread zig-zag along the twisting gorge like a broken snake.

But then we heard the revving of an engine, a sound as sweet as a wail at a birth. The water-wagon was alive again. The black cloud lifted, and we were on the march. Then the cliffs fell away; a salty tang blew crisply on the breeze; the air took on a strange moist chill—and the horizon, so long a pink-grey haze, was suddenly a sharp-edged cobalt line.

It was the sea. Rounding a spur of a yellow-brown shingle ridge we were all at once in full view of, and frighteningly close to, a town—the first town we had seen since Sayun, seven hundred road miles behind us. And once again we were grateful to our Qamsiti defector and Sulayim's secret services. For with a swift wrench of the wheel and a vigorous jab on the throttle we swung up to the right, slithering up the slopes of shingle, and before we had time to contemplate the town or its inhabitants to contemplate us, we were on top of a terrace looking down on Ghaidha. The Jizza disembogued darkly on our left, from out of a haunted-looking valley, and if we had come that way we must have passed almost under the eaves of the outermost buildings. Now, as the purple evening dropped on to us from the east, we sat on our ridge and panted. We were there: we had reached Ghaidha, intact and immaculate.

Gunboat had made it.

M

SIXTEEN

"His Highness Regrets..."

WE sat on our pebbly dais and gazed at the strange town below. While the soldiers wrestled behind us with canvas flapping in the evening breeze, transforming the naked shingle flats into a village of tents, I had nothing to do but survey the capital city of the Mahra mainland.

My first impression was of a giant's cemetery, a great grave-yard of huge crumbling tombs; and then it looked like a city of Sumerian ruins, mouldering mustily on the dusty plain, a dead place, an abode of ravens. For the only living things to be seen were rows of black bird-like figures perched upon the para-pets. The town seemed entirely made up of tall crumbling eyeless castles, separated each from its neighbour by a wide gap. There were no houses, that I could see; nothing that one could call a street; only the spaced forts, blank but for tiny holes of doors and windows. I was so fascinated by the spectacle of this town, which was less a town than a settlement of mutually-warring tenements, that it was some time before the ravens finally evolved into what they really were: women.

And now, first one and then another solitary skulking figure of a man could be seen, dodging furtively between the gaunt walls and diving head-first into a doorway. Soon, too, the flocks of perching women slipped with a flutter down inside their strongholds, and night fell upon a numb, frightened, chillingly unresponsive Ghaidha.

It is clear enough in retrospect that if we had charged straight into the place on arrival, that first evening, we could have taken a fort or two and planted our flag on it. But there would certainly have been resistance, albeit more a reflex counter-punch than serious defence, from the few permanent denizens. And although the troops would have won, the principle that had brought us here bloodless would never have survived unviolated among those crumbling but still solid castles. At that stage, too, we had no knowledge of which castle belonged to whom. It would have been ridiculous to launch our strength against the imposing-looking home of some small and mild-mannered clan; nor did the colonel see any advantage, military or political, in getting his feet stuck in a mud-hole for the sake of waving a flag. So our watchword was Fabius Cunctator. Sooner or later, if we sat there patient on our platform, the ice would break, sooner or later the tribes must come—in peace or in war—to observe the phenomenon of an army encamped above their town. Until then, we were prepared to stare the Mahra out.

Johnson had disposed his troops with care, and our position was impregnable to all but the most skilled and determined of Bedouin guerrillas. When the sun came up the next day we were strongly entrenched. The guides and companions had been set out on a flank, to insulate them from any assault upon our military camp and to establish a meeting-place outside the perimeter where future parleys might take place. Our entourage included a generously-equipped medical team, and we hoped thus to entice at least the sick and the lame, the women and the young, in these early days to call on us.

We had no delusions about the security of the road we had just travelled. We were cut off by land. Our first consignment of rations and petrol was to come by sea from Mukalla, and the R.A.F. had agreed to support us thereafter with a regular air-lift until the road was open. Half-way back to the frontier lay Pat Gray and his men at Murayt, charged with the delicate task of making friends with the tribes in that part of the country. He too was isolated, and must rely for supplies on the Air Force.

So we faced the first morning at Ghaidha, our Gunboat securely tied up to moorings.

Behind us the tawny shingle plateau stretched far along the coast. We could not be surprised from the rear. On our right the terrace fell away to the beach, where a small unlovely fishing village lurked sulkily out of sight. Before us erupted the weird excrescence of Ghaidha, reminding me now of some pustular disease, the forts swelling up over a wide expanse of salty-looking ground. The universal brown was broken by a few splashes of green where helots of the Mahra raised lucerne, millet, and tobacco. Behind and beyond Ghaidha a wide dry watercourse wound down towards us from a distant damson-coloured mountain range which faded, blue and misty, away to the frontiers of Oman. And on the left the lazy Jizza dragged its watery path, exhaustedly dissipating itself before reaching the town.

The Jizza, we learnt soon, was entirely impassable for wheeled traffic. A broad barrier of jagged rocks lay across its gorge about half-way between Murayt and the sea. A vision of Gunboat's fate, impaled on the rocks, invested by the vindictive Kilshat, sent a shudder through my bones. Johnson's instinct had served us well.

Our early attempts to shake hands with Ghaidha were smartly smacked down. Bin Hezhaz, Ashayer, and one or two others of the more pious camp-followers walked down after breakfast towards the mosque, a squat mud hut standing apart. They were gaily confident. The miserable mosque, they said, like the even more wretched bazaar, was neutral ground, a sanctuary where the perpetually warring Mahra could meet and talk and relax among their foes for a precious hour or two. So the small pilgrimage set off to make a few useful contacts in between obeisances to Allah. But as we watched they were intercepted by a trio of armed men who stopped them in their tracks and turned them back, with much gesticulation. The worshippers were outraged, but there was nothing we or they could do. Bin Hezhaz in particular, who enjoyed a country-wide reputation for sanctity and gentle wisdom, felt the blow badly. If even he could not meet the townsmen, even in the mosque, where and when in heaven's name were we to start?

Then the supply dhow arrived. We could see it riding at anchor a few hundred yards out from the beach. The problem was to unload it. Presumably Mukalla had imagined us now to be in full control of Ghaidha and its environs, the grateful liberated Mahra flocking to our flag. Johnson did what he must. He took a patrol down to the fishing village and invited fishermen of goodwill to assist us with the task, for a generous consideration. But even the lure of pelf failed to ensnare the villagers, who were vassals of the lordly Kilshat and lived from day to day in mortal dread of that tribe. So the soldiers commandeered the boats. So the fishermen hid their oars.

Undismayed, the colonel caused oars to be made out of pieces of board and assorted driftwood, and the less landlubberly of the legionaries unloaded the dhow, under the resentful eyes of the fishermen. These promptly served us with a writ, demanding compensation for the misappropriation of, and notional damage to, their boats. I issued a reply saying that the Government was graciously prepared and indeed pleased to discuss this and any other matter with them and anybody else, provided that they came to talk to us. Three years later this commitment came home to roost. It took that time for the oppressed villagers to shake off their shackles and assert what we ourselves had been ready to admit as their right.

Surprisingly, I suffered a considerable verbal battering from our own Mahra—including even Sulayim—for this piece of necessary requisitioning. Some residue of the Mahra soul, some persistent essence of their tribal character impelled them to protest—they, who above all were now manifestly detested by the natives of this place, and dependent for their very lives upon the maintenance of the garrison.

Was it right, asked Sulayim, that the Government should seize innocent fishermen's boats against their will?

I found it hard to argue my case. If you were dying of thirst in the desert, I asked them, and you came upon a man with fresh camels and you asked him for help and he refused, would you lie there in the sand and die upholding the camelman's right to refuse—or would you take a camel, offering at the same time due payment, and returning the animal unharmed as soon as you could?

Sulayim, and Ashayer and Bashayer and the rest, muttered non-committally. I think their main argument, invisibly submerged inside their own schizophrenic minds now torn asunder by divided loyalties, was that we were wrong to further oppress a heavily burdened helot people rather than first exercising our power against the cruel feudal barons of Ghaidha. But Johnson and I could hardly have been expected to interpret fully the subtleties of Ghaidha society so soon after our arrival; and the dhow, after all, must be unloaded.

Meanwhile the spectacle below us presented a mad travesty of a Wild West show. The tribes came galloping in. About twice a day our camp was alerted by the rattle of gunfire from Ghaidha. Answering shots ripped echoing out of the Jizza, or called distantly from the valley behind the town and the mauve hills beyond. And then they came: a rollicking camel rodeo, all helter-skelter, hell for leather pounding out of the hills, banners of powder-smoke flying in the air and rifle-cracks urging the charge. And as the badmen pelted into town, they were amazingly swallowed up. The squadrons were engulfed wholesale by one or another of the forts: each fort its tribe: until the walls bulged.

Now and then we heard a crackling fusillade rebound between the walls—for each tribal mansion was embattled, less against a common enemy like ourselves (something Ghaidha had not seen for a generation or more) than against its neighbour. When the feud-haunted town was full and bursting, we watched small parties emerge, glancing left and right with rifles at the ready, patrols probing no man's land, covered by watchful picquets on the battlements. Thus the Mahra made their cautious way to mosque or market, where they could breathe at ease and discuss the prodigies of the hour with their fellow-Mahra. And thus, presumably, between praying or shopping, they gradually developed their consensus. Then for the journey home again they reverted to Indian files of commandos, threading their dangerous way through the streets to their own ant-hills.

All the time, while these barbaric comings and goings were enacted on the scene below us, the Mahra, by a strange process of inter-tribal telepathy, assumed and maintained a common front towards us: a cold stiff shoulder.

Early in the game I sent a message down to the main Kilshat fort which we had now identified, offering to talk with their chiefs. They detained my Desert Guard messenger for an insulting length of time, and then he climbed grey-faced up the ridge with the reply that if I was anxious to talk to the Kilshat I should descend, alone and unarmed, and meet them in their stronghold. For their part, they were uninterested in us, and had no intention of making any effort to meet us. Johnson refused to countenance the possibility of my falling hostage, and the dialogue ceased before it had got going.

Later I tried to get in touch with another tribe. A small palaver was arranged, through intermediaries, to take place exactly half-way between our front line and the near edge of the town. Under the guns of the Legion I walked down to the appointed spot and sat on the ground and watched while three tall white figures emerged from one of the blind castles and strolled towards me. Then about a hundred yards from their front door, they set themselves down. I thought they were taking a rest, or perhaps having last minute consultations. But they continued to squat there, seeming well contented to spend the rest of the day waiting for me to approach the range of their own sharpshooters and leave the security of my own. So for perhaps half an hour we sat and gazed at each other across a quarter of a mile of Arabia. Then I stood up: they stood up: solemnly we turned about, and with stately tread made our several ways back to whence we had come.

And that was the end of that.

It soon became tacitly understood, quite by what occult means I no longer remember, that the Mahra would do us no harm provided we left them alone. To preserve their face, they wanted the moment of *rapprochement* when it came to be at their instigation, a gesture of splendid conciliation when they felt like making it. We fell in with this pleasing arrangement, for it harmonised with our own Fabian policy, and before the first week was out the play had been reduced to rules as rigid as diplomatic protocol. We had asked for water and firewood from the town, on repayment, and met stony silence. Our patrols discovered an ample supply of both, a mile or two up the Jizza. We helped ourselves, and not once were our foragers even followed, much less molested. Our companions were still forbidden the mosque, but they found no obstacle to visiting friends in the lower part of the town, where unwarlike Sayids and menials lived. It was not many days before even our soldiers, in mufti, were exploring the sad bazaar, a novel but unrewarding day out for them. The holy men and labourers came up in flocks to exploit our free medical service. But not once did a Mahra tribesman or his family come near us.

The weird truce developed a life of its own. Once a party of homecoming Kilshat blundered unawares straight into the outer perimeter of our camp. Quick on the draw as Jesse James, they fired, before they realised what they had challenged—they were promptly pinned down in a gully by a couple of Brens. Johnson sent a scout car down to nudge them out, gently. Not a single round of supporting fire came our way from the Kilshat in the town: the errant gunmen had broken the rules, and must get out by themselves. There was a hideous moment when a light R.A.F. aircraft landed blithely on the gravel below us, just outside the town, imagining that we were in full occupation. The pilot and passengers stepped out, stretched their arms, and began ambling about taking pictures of Ghaidha's castles towering over them. The battlements blossomed with armed men while our whole garrison stood to and held its breath. But nothing happened. Once again Johnson despatched a scout car, with an urgent invitation to the visitors to get the hell out of it. Graciously, but still unalarmed, the tourists climbed back aboard, taxied, and took off to land safely behind our camp. This was very nearly a grave breach of the weird etiquette: but not quite. To me and the colonel, having regard to the exuberant, reckless, animal-like ferocity of the Mahra youth, this incident was a real token of the truce.

But once Johnson and I took a party of soldiers and a companion or two down to the ghetto of Ghaidha, to where the helots lived under the heel of the tyrannous tribes. That was all right: as long as we went straight there and came straight back . . . but on our return we strayed across the frontage of one of the more bellicose clans of Mahra, who smartly let rip at us with a volley of well-aimed shot. Luckily they caught us in dead ground, but to move out of it would invite a further visitation of flying lead. Johnson reluctantly restrained his angry troops from retaliating, and sent instead a delegation of companions to arrange a cease fire. The legionaries were seething, and I felt the lash of the colonel's tongue, for the little jaunt had been my idea. But this time, it was we who had broken the rules.

We had almost forgotten that our pretext for invading the Mahra was the imminent State Visit of their Sultan. We knew that none of the Mahra believed he was coming, and we knew too that they knew of our own disbelief. But having begun the charade we had to play it to its close. My passport came under scrutiny by neutral emissaries of the Kilshat. They agreed that it appeared to embody the permission of the Sultan for Mister Allfree to Travel in Mahra. But, they said, it made no mention of Colonel Johnson, of Colonel Gray, of four hundred soldiers. So once again, and for the last time, the sad little document was folded away out of sight. And all the time the questions flooded in, via one or another of a succession of reluctant slaves or Sayids. If the Sultan was really coming, why had he not sent word to the tribes? Why had he allowed—if (sinisterly) he had indeed allowed—this military outrage? Why, above all, was he not here in person to explain to the tribes that he had invited the Government to drive roughshod through the hallowed land?

I was helpless against this barrage of an inquisition. The Sultan's visit was highly speculative; but in its way, even as a fiction it served our purpose. As long as we could maintain that our whole enterprise lay under the Sultan's blessing, was even at his command, the tribes had a face-saving excuse for not trying harder to expel us. Indeed, as the day of his supposed arrival drew closer, Johnson and I began to see horrid visions of the mad monarch stepping ashore and absolutely disclaiming us and our presence in Ghaidha—a thing which, from past experience, we knew he was quite liable to do.

Then came Arthur Watts. His bulging frame bursting with confidence and *bonhomie* he climbed out of his aeroplane and breezily told me to summon the tribes.

My picture of the situation, the mutual cold shoulders, the rigidly ritualised truce, shook him momentarily, but he was not the man to stay shaken for long. " Summon all the Mahra you can," said he.

I convoked the pathetic assembly : Sulayim, Bin Hezhaz, our few Desert Guards and other camp followers.

Undiscouraged, Arthur Watts proceeded to bestow upon this exiguous gathering the full glory of his eloquence, trusting shrewdly that his words and their emphasis would nevertheless reach his absent audience.

" His Highness regrets he's unable to come today." That was the verse and the refrain of the R.A.'s opening speech. Like Caesar to the Senate, the Sultan would not come to Ghaidha : no reason given—he would not, as was his privilege. The Mahra nodded in complete understanding. The charade must be played out. Perhaps, said Watts, the Sultan would come later on. The Mahra wagged their heads. Perhaps, they echoed.

Then the R.A. produced his Ace of Trumps. Out of his briefcase he drew a photostat document. So important was this paper, he said, so secret, so irreplaceable, that only a photograph could be permitted to leave the archives of Aden.

At once his stock fell. Sophisticated tribunals accept photostats as next best evidence of the original. Mahra, in Al Nissi's words, " are Bedouin—show us the signature." Deep suspicion descended upon Arthur Watts's photograph.

This discredited piece of paper was dramatic enough. It was a letter from the Sultan to the High Commissioner in Aden requesting him to establish and maintain an administration in his mainland territory. Deprived of the radiance of His Highness's physical presence, this was really the best the R.A. could do, and he spent most of the morning explaining the infallibility of modern photographic technique and the unassailable validity of the reproduction in his hand. In the end he overbore the Mahra doubts, and they hazily accepted the thing as a true embodiment of the Sultan's will. But . . . .

" But," they said—and these were an audience of allies— " but there is no word here about granting permission for soldiers to invade the land of the Mahra."

Watts appealed to their logical faculty, urging them to see that the implementation of the Sultan's wish was impossible without the military presence, that the one was inherent in the other. But the Mahra mind, when it chooses, can curl up like an armadillo and present an exterior impenetrable to logic. It was absurd : these men had voluntarily cast their lot with us from the start : but the legality of their role was a thing they would not accept, however persuasively advocated. Perhaps this was a sign, less of their obtuseness than of their perspicacity.

Whatever the cause, in his disguise as *deus ex machina* Arthur Watts had failed to achieve a denouement. His visit was a shot in the arm for the soldiers, and it gave a boost like an after-burner to the morale of myself and my faithful companions, who were beginning to feel as lonely and pointless as Scott on his last haul from the South Pole. Such was the effect of a descent from Olympus. But the barrier of solid ice between the benefactors on their ridge and the barbarians in their forts persisted, unshattered and diamond hard.

The greatest nuisance at Ghaidha were the flies—far more of a pest than the Mahra. Ghaidha knew not the smallest vestige of sanitary practice or theory, beyond the most basic biological principles. The inhabitants in time of peace used the vast stretch of Arabia that lay around them. But when the tribes were embattled, as now, inside their several fastnesses, with perhaps a hundred alimentary canals at work within one three-storey mud cell, the problem was more delicate. It was solved simply, by the accumulation of a huge dunghill at the back of each tenement. The flies buzzed around in thick black clouds, and they needed no more than a day to discover the fresh delights of our new and latrineless camp. Up they hummed in joy, to settle upon us like a black snowstorm. They clustered in sooty deposits on the tent roofs, they turned the tent ropes into strings of black beads. Unless one maintained a perpetual tic of twitching eyelids, nostrils, and lips, they could quickly make a man's face look like the side of a busy beehive. Worst of all was trying to eat. I used to hold my plate of rice in my left hand, jammed hard against my mouth, and fan it with a fork. Then seizing my moment I plunged the fork with a desperate stab into the rice and hoped to jab the mouthful between my clenched lips and resume the fanning before the buzzing plague could get a toe in. Half the time I had a clear round. When I was bested I consoled myself with the thought of the fate awaiting the flies inside me.

Perhaps to beguile our tedious days with a spot of light relief, the Sultan sent us his executioner, all the way from Socotra. This functionary turned out to be a mild-looking black man of jelly-like consistency and surprising charm though small of intellect, and he thoroughly enjoyed his holiday from the daily round of judicial amputation on the island. We had few enough diversions. Eric Johnson took out patrols each day to explore the country, making no friends. The mutual despatch to Coventry became a way of life. I stared at Ghaidha and meditated on the wonder of the place: here was a town, with people living in it; with buildings kept in a basic state of repair; with a street of shops and fields of greenery irrigated with diesel pumps, for which oil was imported and a mechanic retained—and there was not the merest wisp of authority, not even the titular shadow of a municipal government, no more law than the ancient customs of the tribes. There was not even the mutual good-neighbourliness that might keep a city of Utopia from chaos—the most noticeable feeling in Ghaidha was mutual hatred and fear. Ghaidha was unalloyed anarchy, a settlement of ungoverned men in their most unbridled condition. Ghaidha was a phenomenon.

One last note echoes in my ears from those crazy days. A group of Kilshat had lately come home from working overseas, and their curiosity overcame the tribal veto and they wandered up one day to inspect us. They bore strange news from out of Africa—this was November, 1963, when East Africa was in the throes of Uhuru.

" Africa is going down the drain," they said in effect. " You know what's happening? The Christians have been beaten, and the slaves are taking over."

My contract expired before the ice broke. After two weeks of staring at the frozen town below, I packed up and waved farewell to Eric Johnson, to Sulayim, to the Desert Guards and the flies. It was nearly ten years since I had first set foot in Arabia. The great days were past. The sober civil servants, the starry-eyed latter-day Lawrences, the mercenaries like myself and Gray and Johnson, all could see the " mene mene " on the wall. Dropping Hassan off in Sayun, I left Arabia for good.

Epilogue

Après nous le déluge. About two days after my departure, some of the Mahra—not the Kilshat—chose to break the truce. They opened fire from their fort at a routine patrol and killed a couple of soldiers. All the pent-up wrath, all the frustrated fury of the Legion was at last let off the leash by Colonel Johnson. He launched them at the offending quarter of the town and smartly he punished it. The Kilshat and the others looked on impassive: it was a trial of strength, the first real test of the fist we had kept so long in its soft glove. And it was a triumph. The offending tribe was expelled summarily from their fort, leaving half a dozen dead behind, and the Legion seized the noisome building and kept it. At last the red and white flag flew over Ghaidha. The lesson was well learnt. That was the first and the last time the Mahra kicked against the traces.

After that explosion, the freeze slowly but steadily thawed. Three years after Gunboat's dropping anchor, the army and the Political Officer were still encamped in their fly-pestered tents on the yellow shingle terrace; but a strong fort was under construction, to dominate the sordid settlement of Ghaidha for evermore. My successor was a chunky ex-policeman named Bob Clarke, during whose reign the first steps were taken to establish a Mahra Tribal Council. In the days of Gunboat such a move was just a mad dream; but it came to pass, with Sulayim prominent in its deliberations (the cloak of secrecy enshrouding his office was in the course of time shrugged off and he thereafter served the Government, still deviously, but openly). The Sultan never came, but he sent a brother, a man small of stature and smaller of character, to chair the council. The chiefs of the Kilshat co-operated in the founding and building of this unbelievable parliament, and the Khowar and other half-digested Kathiris began to take an interest.

And Ghaidha incredibly became a regular port of call for Aden Airways Limited, and is even marked on the maps as an airport.

All this came about through the continued magic influence of the word " oil ". The American company whose activities had precipitated the invasion packed up one day with almost indecent haste and departed, but the lure of oil is a powerful one and not long passed before another company stepped into their shoes. The new concession was almost entirely concentrated within the putative boundaries of the Mahra Sultanate, and no longer was there any point in Rashid, Khowar or Bin Duwais cavilling at their possible subjection to Socotra. The other Sultans now had little to offer them. They doffed their Kathiri pride with careless abandon and evinced no distaste for the despised garments of the Mahra. Even the Manahil nibbled at the idea that their better interests might be served by joining this galloping bandwagon.

The years following my farewell to Arabia wrought many changes among the characters of my story. Pat Gray was murdered by his own sentry, while returning home from the Residency at Mukalla. The atrocity was private, not political, but its foul nature, and the courage shown by Gray in driving his wounded wife to hospital while the life ebbed out of him, affected the small community of Mukalla as much as if it had been the first blow of a reign of terror. Pat Gray's second in command had been murdered similarly the year before, at Murayt, and Eric Johnson personally took over the Hadhrami Bedouin Legion.

Arthur Watts retired and took his violin to soothe the sleepy hills of Sussex. Jim Ellis became R.A. as the culmination of sixteen years' service to the Government and people of the Protectorate. Aunty Hussein was sacked from his State Secretaryship in Sayun, and Sayid Ali retired gracefully from the Ministry of Education, both men having been adjudged too cobwebby for the 1960s. Musellem, that professional bankrupt who had tried to dig my wells, found himself involved financially in a venture of politically subversive character and finally achieved the goal to which he had so long apparently aspired: a prison cell. The Qaiti Sultan died of his immeasurably complex assortment of diseases, physical and mental, and was succeeded by his English-educated son. Hassan my cook set up business as a brewer of illicit liquor.

To the desert, and the Bedouin, the coming of the British was a small whim of God. There is something enduring about the huge sand dunes, the endless empty horizons, the foul water and solitary wandering camels and the sublimely arrogant Bedouin soul. The Romans, the Abyssinians, the Turks, the British have all in their turn come, and in their turn have gone. Whoever comes next will leave as shallow an imprint. The Saar and Rashid and the Mahra have seen it all, and they have doubtless a great deal more to see. But they will remain Saar and Rashid and Mahra, and hate each other to the end of time.